Alaskan Aberration

The View from a Harley in the North Country

by

Allen J Bartell

FLAT
BLACK
Publishing

Alaskan Aberration
The View from a Harley in the North Country

Published by

FLAT
BLACK
Publishing

Rt 2 Box 25-C
Trinity, TX 75862
1-800-707-1015

Copyright © 1997 Allen J. Bartell
First Printing 1997

Cover photo by Joan Swim.

Library of Congress Catalog Card Number: 97-61413

ISBN: 0-9659752-0-7

Printed in the USA by

MP

Morris Publishing
3212 East Highway 30 • Kearney, NE 68847 • 1-800-650-7888

Alaskan Aberration

The View from a Harley in the North Country

\ **ab-er-ra-tion**\ *n* the act of deviating from what is normal or natural, esp. from a moral standard.

If
you will
practice being fictional
for a while, you will understand
that fictional characters are
sometimes more real than
people with bodies
and heartbeats.

-Richard Bach
Illusions

Introduction

> *Like a blast of foul air the roar of a Harley pierces the night. Before you can focus on him, the mysterious rider is gone. The drone of his engine fading in the darkness and the glowing coal of his tail light are the only proof that he was real. Your mind drifts, wondering what it would be like to be truly free, free of society's standards, free of obligation, free to travel through the landscape without obstruction.*

A popular Harley Davidson T-shirt says, "If I have to explain, you wouldn't understand." People often ask me what touring on my Harley is like. I tell them it is hard to describe, complex. But contrary to that T-shirt, I have attempted to define it by taking you with me to Alaska on my Harley. I have ridden motorcycles since I was twelve, but didn't really discover motorcycling until just before my twentieth birthday. That summer, I left the sanctuary of my parent's home and explored the backroads of New Mexico and Colorado on a second hand Suzuki. I discovered the joys of traveling on a motorcycle—an education far beyond that offered in any university.

Touring on a motorcycle is a unique experience. On a bike you have a panoramic view, seeing and feeling more. Exposure to the elements, being at the mercy of mother nature, added to the thrill and danger of speed, creates a stimulating adrenaline rush. It is a constant exhilaration, like a high that creates no hangover, has no side effects and goes on as long as you ride. The people you meet, the things you see, and the events that occur all combine to add depth to the trip. When you are on a motorcycle loaded with camping gear, people are drawn to you; exploring their similarities and differences is part of the thrill.

But it is far more than this; for if it wasn't then being on a bike would be little different than traveling in the family mini-van with the doors and windows wide open. Riding brings out a different personality, the fictional character within you. While you are moving there is nobody to talk to and nobody to listen to. The wind blocks out all other sounds. This leaves you alone with your thoughts. A sort of meditation, but meditation while stimulated rather than in relaxation. Your thoughts come quickly, easily, and aggressively. Often they **are** aggressive. You become a whole new person, confident, invincible, even immortal. The danger makes it seem even more real. The old cliché applies, "You are never more alive than when you are closest to death." I know now why bikers are so infatuated with tattoos depicting death. It is also why outlaws like the Hell's Angels, along with the current wave of yuppie riders, have chosen motorcycles as their means of transportation and even existence. The bike has allowed them to become the mysterious anomaly we have all contemplated, disappearing into the darkness.

If my writing seems cocky or self centered it is the result of the culmination of these aspects of riding. I not only wanted to put you in the seat but also inside my head to see how a bike liberates and changes your personality.

This trip has additional factors to consider. Exhaustion and depression are added to the equation, creating a whole new range of emotions and thoughts. Also the overpowering beauty of the Northern wilderness creates an awesome sense of joy and wonderment. In short the whole trip becomes a roller coaster of emotions, unpredictable and reckless, always keeping you on your toes and wondering what might come next.

I always keep a journal during my trips. I chose to stick with that format to stay true to the experience. I did not write a story. I recorded the events, the thoughts, and the emotions that occurred along the highway as they happened, not as I remember them. I hope you will enjoy and appreciate them as much as I do.

Allen J. Bartell

June 23, Trinity, Texas

Today I'm northbound. All of my belongings are stacked in a small dank shed, my checkbook and bills have been turned over to my parents. For the next two months I have no obligations, no bills, nobody to answer to; I am going to Alaska. The only things that are not in the shed are on my bike: a change of clothes, rain gear, a tent, a sleeping bag, a cooking stove, and some miscellaneous odds and ends. These necessities, packed into a tour pack weigh down my Sportster. Yes, you heard it I'm going to Alaska on an 883 cc Harley, modified with a windshield, a five gallon fat bob gas tank, and a trunk off a touring bike. Costing half as much as other models, Sportsters aren't even considered "real" Harleys by many bikers who ride the heavy weight 1340 cc Harley "big twins." Most people think I'm crazy, taking a sport bike on a long distance road trip, but it's all I have and nothing is going to keep me from taking this trip. I think I am "hard core" but will soon find out that I'm not as tough as I think.

Two years ago I decided to get rid of my Yamaha and buy a Harley. When you buy a Harley you are getting more than a motorcycle, you are buying into a lifestyle, a subculture. No other group of bikers has such a strong sense of camaraderie. People who would probably not even be seen together under any other circumstances become the best of friends as fellow Harley riders. I envied that fraternal feeling and wanted to become a part of it. At the same time I decided that I needed to create some sort of adventure for myself before I became entrenched in some job that I couldn't escape or found myself married. It only made sense to incorporate my bike into the adventure. My destination? Australia . . . too expensive. Mexico . . . I don't speak Spanish. Antarctica . . . no roads. Alaska . . . Alaska . . . the Alaskan Highway! Yes! Pictures of pristine wilderness, snowcapped peaks, bears, and treacherous gravel roads filled my head. My mind was made up. All that was left was the planning.

My bike feels heavy and slow as I pull away. It seems like a completely different machine with all the luggage but I'll get used to it. As I work my way through the gears and up to highway speed, I can't help but smile. Having no idea what lies ahead, I embrace uncertainty. Riding up I-45 with the temperature rising, I can't wait to escape the damned East Texas heat and humidity. Born and raised in South Dakota, I will never adjust to 90 degrees and 90 percent humidity. The sticky air smells of decay and is heavy, like fluid in my lungs. But the heat is not all I'm escaping. I teach inner city fifth graders at a residential school. I eat with kids. I sleep with kids. For nine months out of every year, eighty hours a week, I think of little except kids. My Harley is my escape. On weekends I ride. On my bike I'm not a teacher with strict moral standards. I'm just another anomic biker in black leather. I have almost complete anonymity. Conversations between bikers rarely turn to occupation. It is almost taboo to discuss your work. Non-bikers never ask about your career, they want to believe you are simply a biker; a modern day cowboy. I am happy to fulfill their romantic delusion. But this trip is more than a weekend retreat. I have been saving for two years. I'm acting out the Peter Fonda, *Easy Rider* fantasy. Living on the road with nothing but my bike for support, exposed to all the elements, sleeping on the ground, going wherever the road takes me. I will not discuss my job. I *am* simply a biker.

Riding is an intense experience, the wind turns sound into a continuous explosion and drives every smell deep into your face. At sixty miles per hour raindrops become pebbles and pebbles become bullets when they hit your face. The vibration blurs your vision yet you see more, every bump in the road, every car that could cut in front of you, every tree and sign that comes flying by, the ground below, the sky above; you see more. With the road flying by right beneath, it is easy to see why many bikers refer to their machines as sleds.

Riding through some construction, I notice a sign politely stating, "Motorcycles Use Extreme Caution." Not wanting to die, I always use caution. My senses are tuned in to everything around and in front, anything that could pose a hazard on the highway or any signal that my bike could develop a problem. My life depends on it. On a bike the slightest malfunction is enough to send you sliding down the highway to your death, slamming you into any solid object that lies in front or leaving you in the path of the next truck that waits to flatten you from behind. Riding enclosed in their cars, most people forget that driving is dangerous, potentially fatal. On a bike you never forget, but you don't dwell on it; it is simply part of the thrill.

"We must not demean life by standing in awe of death."
-David Sarnoff

"Avoiding danger is no safer in the long run than outright exposure. Life is either a daring adventure or nothing."
-Hellen Keller

Suddenly a Dodge Ramcharger with a collage of bumper stickers snaps me back to reality. "Insured by Glock," "Some People are Alive Simply Because it is Illegal to Kill Them," and "Is your church approved by the BATF?" We live in a free country as long as we conform to an unwritten set of standards, if we stray to far from the norm the system will find a way to put us down. This trip is a way for me to assert my freedom. I tend to stay within society's boundaries but hope there will always be some who don't.

"One wonders what would happen in a society in which there were no rules to break, doubtless everyone would quickly die of boredom."
-Susan Howatch

Soon, oaks and cedars replace the familiar loblolly pines. Dallas suddenly looms ahead and my stomach starts churning. I have never been able to adjust to the stresses of city life and specifically city driving. The next hour is spent dodging cars and trucks. Concentrating on the traffic, I fail to notice the heat rising up from under my seat. Outside of the city limits, I realize that not only is the heat of my engine baking me from below, but the sun is burning me from above. I forgot sunscreen. In a way I want to burn my face, to look tough, hard core. A hard core look to match my hard core destination. That is one of the reasons I'm doing this trip, for my ego. When people look at me I want them to think, "Wow, I'll bet that guy has been around." When people give me a hard time about having a Sportster instead of a "real" Harley, I want to show them my odometer and say, "Has your 'real' Harley seen this kind of mileage." I now realize that my face and arms need protection. A convenience store has some cheap stuff that makes my skin itch and break out, but it protects my bare arms and face from the carcinogenic radiation that threatens me from above.

The oaks and cedars have now surrendered to open grasslands; the only trees are those that have been planted to block the incessant winds. The same bleak scenery confronts me for the next thousand miles. Rolling hills with small farms wrapped in shelter belts, hiding in the valleys. A red barn and a couple of silos, they all look the same. Through Oklahoma, Kansas, Nebraska, and the Dakotas there is little change. Actually these grasslands continue into Canada. Sometimes it feels like they never end.

By the time the road crosses the Red River into Oklahoma the heat is unbearable. I am constantly squirting myself with my water bottle to keep cool. My oil tank is too hot to touch, my butt will be a baked ham by the end of the day. Stopping at a rest area to celebrate my escape from Texas, I pull out my bed roll and decide to wait till the cool of night to travel on. As soon as I lie down a couple on an old Harley shovelhead pulls up. The bike is loud and beat up, lots of personality, sleeping bags and other gear hanging everywhere. They offer me a joint, I smoke a cigar instead but we end up talking. Rick the Prick and Dee-Dee from San Antonio; they make an odd couple. Rick has a gaunt dark leathery face marked with scars, obscured by dirty stubble. Dee-Dee is small but full figured with a clean face lit by a childish smile. They talk me into riding with them rather than waiting for night. After about an hour's rest we are back on the road again. Riding without a bra, Dee-Dee turns heads in many of the cars we pass, her white blouse hiding very little. Rick seems to enjoy showing her off. We ride together to Oklahoma City where they have reserved a camp site at a Kampground Of America, complete with a swimming pool and game room. KOAs cater to RVs and family campers, offering a sterile, non-threatening, city park atmosphere. I had vowed not to camp at a single KOA and here I am on my first night. It will be my last in one.

June 24, Oklahoma City

We get up early and ride hard in the cool morning air. Rick and Dee-Dee are headed to Salina, Kansas for a family reunion, "They're gonna shit when they see us pull in on the bike." Rick seems pretty hard-core. A small automatic pistol hides in his boot. His tattoo says, "Only Death is Certain" next to the grim reaper, but he thinks KOAs are Heaven on Earth.

Before we get out of Oklahoma the superheated wind scalds our lungs and sears our eyes. I alternate closing my eyes and holding my breath to relieve the agony. When we pull into a truck stop to fuel up I listen to my engine idle for a minute. The loud chattering alarms me, it sounds like rapid asthmatic breathing. We are forced to stop every half hour to cool ourselves and the bikes under whatever shade we can find along the burning highway. Lying under a shelter on a picnic table near the Kansas border I watch the clouds changing shape, something I haven't done since I was a child. A thunderbird and dog appear; as a child I saw whole action adventure stories. *That's an alligator splashing water on two kids in a canoe. Do you see it?* As adults we tend to lose that kind of creativity.

Rick interrupts my daydream with a critique of my bike, "Why do you drive with your headlight on?"

"It comes on automatically when I start it, so people can spot me easier."

He responds with a cocky voice, "I put a switch on mine so I can run with it off. I ride assuming nobody can see me; I don't need a light. The only thing I count on is myself."

What he really means is he rides without a light so others can tell he has a Harley. If you ever see a bike without a headlight, it is probably a Harley. It is sort of a signal. I would rather be more visible. If someone can't figure out that my bike is a Harley, I don't care.

He continues to study my machine, "You still have factory mufflers! Where are your drag pipes?"

"These new engines run better with a little back pressure in the pipes, you actually lose power with non-restricting drag pipes."

14

Without realizing his contradiction he exclaims, "Loud pipes save lives!" He wants people to hear his bike but doesn't want them to see him. Not wanting to offend him, I keep my smile hidden.

He is relieved to find out that I have punched holes in my mufflers so my bike has a good loud "Harley" rumble. All I have to do is crack my throttle and everybody knows I'm here.

After one good long run of about 70 miles, we stop at a dilapidated bar in Salina, Kansas. It is marked by no name, just a Schlitz beer sign stating "On Tap." Walking into the small red shack feels like entering a bomb shelter, retreating from the blasting heat. The bar is dark inside with a crimson glow coming through red drapes. All the fixtures and posters are stained yellow from years of smoky conversation. A Hamms beer sign has moving lights attempting to give the river in the picture a realistic flow. I remember seeing these signs as a kid in Dakota. Little has changed in this place for years. The ancient bartender sits lifeless in a high-backed chair at the end of the bar. He hobbles down after a few minutes and I order a beer with tomato juice. "Red" beers are a midwestern standard, Rick nods in agreement. He tries to talk me into staying with them at the local KOA but I told my folks that I would be in Dakota tomorrow. I need to put on more miles tonight.

Before crossing the Nebraska border, I am greeted with familiar Midwest smells, cottonwoods, prairie potholes, chaff from combines, and the stench of barnyards. The deserted farms with their majestic trees and lilacs still blooming, smell more alive than the working farms with the smell of manure and decay. The modern farms are no longer homes like they used to be. Most are now simply corporate factories.

In serious conservative country now, billboards exclaim: "Abortion Kills", "Save a Whale Be a Hero, Save a Baby Go to Jail", and "Freedom of Religion, not Freedom from Religion." Some people would have everybody in the U.S. declare a religion before becoming a citizen. I am religious but against organized religion. If people would spend less time putting each other into categories and spend more time seeking diversity, we would have fewer problems in this country. Liberal or Conservative, Libertarian or Socialist, Republican

15

or Democrat, I am not any of these. Looking at each issue independently, I make up my own mind instead of categorizing myself and then letting that category form my opinions.

"We have just enough religion to make us hate,
but not enough to make us love one another."
-Swift

I stop at the Nebraska border to put on my helmet. Like Texas, Nebraska thinks it has to protect my safety by passing helmets laws. A helmet could save my life in a wreck but it distracts from the experience. I ride for the thrill, the high, and so anything that distracts from it is a liability. Helmets cut off most of the sound and put an enormous strain on my neck. In fact, many people are killed by helmets, the extra weight on their heads snapping their necks in an accident. I harm nobody by riding without a helmet; I just want to have that choice.

I put on my jacket too, not because I need it but because I hope to need it as the sun drops in the west. Covered with patches it does more than protect, it expresses my individuality. Harley patches share space with an armadillo, Mickey Mouse, and a peace symbol. On the back I proudly display a misquote from Frost, "I chose the road less traveled and that has made all the difference."

Near Hebron, Nebraska the red sunset is split by a long, narrow, dark cloud. The cloud is not alarming but unusual. Passing underneath, a cold wind slaps me in the face. Suddenly a freezing rain soaks me. This sudden change in temperature sends my body into shock. The sun is still shining and the raindrops seem alive as they sparkle and jump off the highway. Then, as quickly as it started, it is over. The wind quickly dries my legs. It is peacefully calm and warm, but not as warm as before. Things look different, not just clean like after any thunderstorm, but different. A brilliant rainbow in the east challenges the firey sunset in the west. The sky above is an eerie shade of deep blue-green, like watercolors that have all been mixed together by a child. Fields of ripe yellow wheat blind my eyes while the headlights of the approaching cars shine like blue jewels. I hope all of my trip will be as unique as this stretch of Highway 81 that I have traveled at least twenty times before.

A car passes me with "Rapid City or Bust" painted with shoe polish on the back window. For them South Dakota is a destination, an adventure. I have no definite destination. I plan on making it to Alaska but if not, I will still have an adventure. It is all relative, I will never climb Mount Everest but I make every little trip on my bike exciting. I rarely plan my routes, I don't care. I like to look at every little thing as if it has never happened before.

> "A traveler sees what he sees, a tourist
> sees what he has come to see."
> -Gilbert Chesterson

I am definitely a traveler.

A huge neon red 'S' perched on top of a grain elevator announces Stromsberg, Nebraska. I set up my camp in a quaint city park in this quaint Scandinavian town, free of charge. Sore and tired, I sleep next to the Blue River without interruption as high school kids cruise through the park sharing their loud music with me.

June 25, Stromsberg, Nebraska

I wake up and relieve myself on a nearby tree without bothering to put on my boots. Returning to the tent, my feet are soaked. Looking across the grass I notice that upon each blade rests a large drop of dew. Looking toward the sunrise, I see a tiny rainbow caught in each drop. The blazing orange sun overpowers the red 'S' on the elevator. Surrounded by beautiful colors, I dry my feet and slip on my boots. After walking without them, I realize how much they confine my feet.

Worried about the effects of yesterday's heat, I ride through the morning cool listening to every sound my bike makes, trying to hear whatever it is trying to tell me. I feel every vibration and bump waiting for any signal it might be trying to give. All I can hear is a polite, "Good morning Al!" followed by a reminder, "I could use some fresh oil." I can handle that. I stop at the Harley dealer in Norfolk, Nebraska to change the oil. They let me do it myself behind their shop, not too many dealers allow that type of thing anymore. If they aren't doing the work, then you don't use the facilities. They blame it on liability, but they make big money on labor charges.

Crossing the Missouri River at Yankton, South Dakota, I see blackbirds with their red wings sparking as they fly, clouds of gnats shapeshifting over potholes, and brome grass waving in the wind; all old friends announcing that I am close to home. At a rest stop near Forestburg, I notice the remnants of days past. Rusty playground equipment sits quietly on the far side of a small creek crossed by a dangerously decaying bridge. Once upon a time people came here to recreate. Now this area is for emergency use only, people who can't wait until the next convenience store to drain their coffee filled bladders. No reason to keep it up since nobody plays here anymore.

In a light sleep, I hear a car pull up. The driver gets out, but instead of going toward the outhouses, the steps come toward me. Cautiously, I open one eye to see an old lady approaching me with a box and a thermos. "Would you like a donut? I work at a shop and these are leftovers from this morning." We eat and drink coffee together, quite a sight to passers by. A nice old lady talking to a dirty biker. She

18

thinks my trip is wonderful and wishes me good luck before she leaves.

A few miles past the rest area the road turns north. Suddenly the wind hits me from the side, I hadn't noticed its strength behind the cover of the trees in the rest area. An hour later, it is coming out of the west so hard that my eardrums begin to hurt. I plug them with toilet paper but it still grates on me.

I make it to my parents' home before dark. After enjoying a hot shower and a great dinner, we discuss my travel plans or lack of them. I lie in my old familiar bed with the cool dry air caressing my sore body and the crickets singing me to sleep.

June 26, Conde, South Dakota

Waking to the sound of a meadowlark directly outside my window, I take a deep breath of the fresh Dakota air without opening my eyes. I feel as though I am immersed in the prairie with no house enclosing me. Opening my eyes surrounded by the room I lived in for eighteen years, I feel like I have never left. This farm will always be my home, no matter where I live.

Our land is no longer worked by my family; my dad retired about ten years ago. The deterioration of the buildings and growth of weeds in the corrals mark the end of the farm that was homesteaded by my ancestors over a hundred years ago. My parents don't notice the decay since they view it on a day by day basis. Visiting once a year, I see the changes more readily. I feel some guilt for not taking over, but these days a family farm is not practical. The future comes in spite of the past and I am not a farmer. My dad understands but he wants me to settle down, find a permanent job, get a house and a family. He thinks that this trip will be an end to my adventures, and the beginning of my "mature" life. He doesn't understand my passionate wanderlust, my love for uncertainty. My mother is worried about the trip, "Won't you be lonely, all by yourself?"

I explain to her, that by traveling alone, I meet more people. On the road, breaking up a conversation between people is uncomfortable, but approaching a solitary individual for companionship is easier, probably natural. I am going to Alaska not only to see the sights, but also to meet the people. The road makes friends out of strangers.

I am also traveling for a certain amount of solitude. Loneliness can be one of the greatest ailments of the soul, while solitude can be one of the greatest cures. Riding with the rumble of my bike soothing me, blocking out all other sounds, leaves me alone with my thoughts mixing in my mind. At its best biking is as pure as Zen meditation, at its worst it is as disturbing as a bad nightmare. Above all, alone on the road is rarely lonely.

Before leaving, I visit Mark Wattier, a friend of the family. He builds custom bikes and helps me get parts. Mark was a biker back when Harley was owned by American Machine and Foundry, AMF, the 1970's and 80's. He rode when riding wasn't as popular as it is today and you had to work on your bike to keep it going. I grew up riding a variety of dirt bikes, but I was always around Harleys. Every Sunday at our little country church, we were joined by members of the local club, the Clark County Riders. They were non-conformists, but were accepted by our community. I remember when Doug Lynch baptized his son "Harley David."

Today, Harley riders are still considered an elite, group but they are no longer non-conformists. The high price of the new bikes, sometimes exceeding $15,000, has excluded most of the old riders, leaving the bikes for doctors and lawyers. Having traveled thousands of miles on Jap bikes, I don't care what somebody rides, I care why they ride. The attitude is everything. I ride for the freedom, for the thrill, and to meet people. Today, many ride to flaunt their wealth.

"Don't call him a biker until you see him ride."

I had hoped Mark would come on this trip but his family comes first; he has a new son. He goes over my gear with me, makes a few wise suggestions, and offers any help if I need it along the way. "I'm just a phone call away."

Heading west, I stop in Redfield to look up a former classmate from high school who is now a deputy sheriff. At the Spink County courthouse I ask about Nick. He is not working, but another deputy gives me an escort to his house rather than give me directions. I wonder if he is doing a background check on me as we drive through town. I don't trust cops, especially on my bike. Cops aren't normal people, they are usually on some sort of power trip with the law on their side. You're alone, on a bike. They can do whatever they want. You have no witnesses and what judge is going to take your word over that of a respected officer? I want no trouble so I give them no excuse. Whenever I'm pulled over, and it happens a lot on a bike, I am all 'sir.' "Yes, Sir." "No, Sir." Nick is not home so I move on to Pierre to spend the night with one of my sisters.

June 27, Pierre, South Dakota

Taking a side trip, I cross the Missouri river over the top of Oahe Dam. Dedicated by President Kennedy this was once the largest earthen dam in the world. Backing up nearly two hundred miles of water, this huge slug destroyed thousands of archaeological sites and miles of prime river bottomland. The green forested valleys were drowned to produce electricity that leaves the state. The lakeshores are on what was once the tops of rocky buttes and are gradually filling the reservoir with silt. Someday this dam will be nothing but a waterfall reminding us of our inability to control nature.

The landscape changes drastically when you cross the Missouri River. Here a definite line separates the East from the West. East of the Missouri is rolling glaciated farm land. Green fields of wheat carpet the ground and shelter belts of trees interrupt the views. West of the Missouri is arid Western topography. Patches of bare, clay hardpan sit around rugged flat topped buttes. Cacti and Yucca begin to appear and the views extend farther and farther. The clean landscape makes anything manmade look completely out of place. As I pass under a power line I duck my head, instinctively, as if it were about to decapitate me.

I see a dead coyote splattered into the highway. Guts and meat lie everywhere. I find the cleanest path and ride through it, hoping I don't get too much decay on my leathers. Roadkill is the highway's grim reminder of our own mortality. Someday that coyote could be me. Maybe they could patch me up but who cares about a coyote? My indifference makes me feel guilty. A few years after I'm gone who will care about me?

After a short stop to eat lunch with my brother, I head west to spend the night with another sister living in the far end of the state. The 200 mile trip to her house takes me over 70 miles of gravel roads and construction in the worst wind I have ever seen outside of a storm. It is blowing over fifty miles per hour straight out of the west. Riding into it, my bike struggles to maintain sixty on the level stretches of highway. Turning perpendicular to the wind, it nearly blows me off the road. Earplugs from Mark keep it from pounding my ear drums, but it assaults my body. I feel like a defenseless child being attacked by an invisible bully—slapping and pushing me from all angles, screaming insults that I can't understand, tormenting me. At an unprotected country gas station it nearly blows my bike over. The powerlines wail and the road signs dance wildly in this torturous wind. This turns out to be one of the hardest rides of my trip, physically.

In spite of the wind, I enjoy increasing wildlife along the highway, especially the herds of pronghorn antelope and mule deer. Both have an interesting gait, reminding me of Pepe le Peu, the romantic skunk of Saturday morning cartoon fame. This bounding run appears awkward but Pronghorn are exceeded in speed only by the cheetah. They are well suited to the dry harsh climate here. In the summer temperatures often exceed 100 F and in the winter sink below -30 F. The Pronghorn were originally migratory. Fencing of the land has interrupted their annual journey. Normally they make it through the winter unaffected. Occasionally an especially tough winter with deep snow and cold temperatures will cause "winter kill," decimating the population. In a couple of years they always bounce back. As I roar past, some groups jump with a start and stampede while others look up with casual indifference or simply ignore me.

I rejoice at the end this wind blown day with a steak dinner at the Corner Cafe in Camp Crook. It amazes me that this town of about fifty people supports a cafe, a good cafe. They serve the best prime rib I have ever eaten.

June 28, Camp Crook, South Dakota

My last day in South Dakota, I hit U.S. Highway 85 forty miles east of Camp Crook in Buffalo. I am quickly passed by a couple on a BMW doing 85 or 90. Stopping for a break north of Belle Fourche at the geographical center of the US, I scan the view from the top of a rocky butte. The highway, dwarfed by the magnitude of the landscape, looks like a black thread tossed carelessly on the ground. The couple on the BMW are still in the parking lot when I come down. Noticing British Columbia plates, I strike up a conversation. I offer them some travel suggestions in the Black Hills and they give me some for Vancouver Island, suggesting I take the Canadian ferry from Prince Rupert to Port Hardy on my return trip. Nearly out of gas, they ask for an escort to Belle Fourche. They make it to the truck stop before running out and we enjoy breakfast together.

Crossing the Wyoming border on I-90, I am surrounded by familiar sights; the Black Hills, Inyan Kara, Devil's Tower, and soon, the Bighorns. Along the cutbank of the highway some sort of archaeologists are digging in the rock, probably looking for bones. A year ago I helped dig a dinosaur from the badlands not far from here, a t-rex. Nothing serious, just a few hours volunteering, enough to satisfy my curiosity and say I did it.

Stopping at a pullout, I fill my lungs with the pungent aroma of sagebrush. A red wash along the road draws me into it. Along the bottom are a few rib bones bleaching in the sun. My mind takes me away imagining all sorts of murder mysteries, wondering whose remains I have just stumbled across. Possibly a hitchhiker or maybe a vagrant Indian who happened to be in the wrong place at the wrong time. I continue down, looking for the skull. Finally, I spot it, a spike mule deer. The only crime here might be failure to report an accident. For some reason, deep in my mind, I know that someday I am going to stumble upon a body, in a roadside park. It seems inevitable to me. Each time I stop and walk to the stall, I carefully peek inside. No body, this time.

I stop to fuel up in Buffalo before beginning my ascent into the mountains. Spotting a red Blazer pulling a trailer with Texas plates, I notice the driver is wearing a Fairbanks T-shirt. After asking him about the Alaskan Highway he looks at my set up and says I have nothing to worry about. He offers me a guidebook to the Alcan. His book proves to be more of a burden than a help. It looks like a phone book and weighs even more. Every possible stop in northern Canada and Alaska is listed. With hindsight I see that it was meant for tourists rather than a traveler.

My bike pulls up to Powder River Pass like a champ. I stop to enjoy the flowers of the alpine tundra, at 9,666 feet. I have always been impressed with plants or anything that survives under adverse conditions. It is not always the biggest or the strongest that survive. Nature rewards creativity, adaptation. The plants of the tundra survive by dwarfing, squatting down to conserve heat and protect themselves from the constant wind. I lay down on my belly and see the inconspicuous survivors struggling to hang on. Flowers that would, anywhere else, raise themselves proudly toward the deep blue sky, hide between the rocks searching for a ray of sunlight. Anything that tries to reach too high here is quickly cut down to size.

I take my first picture here to record the highest altitude of my trip. Taking pictures is fine, but the camera can take over a trip. Many scenes and experiences have been ruined by taking a photo. Sometimes I will get so engrossed in taking the perfect shot that, after leaving, I realize that I never really enjoyed the scene. I just took a photo and moved on. That won't happen on this trip. I will enjoy each view and event and if I think of it, I might take a photo. Photographs of scenery are almost useless. I hear myself saying to the people I show them to, "It was a lot more impressive, bigger. This photo doesn't do it justice." Showing a picture of a mountain does no better job of capturing the spirit than showing a rock from its side. The only advantage of the photo is that it doesn't take anything from the mountain.

I roll off the mountains and slide into Ten Sleep Canyon. The steep winding road hurls me mercilessly into the stark heat of the desert below. At the bottom I take off my jacket and lace it onto my front fork. A carload of Indians pulls off the road behind me. The driver shoots me a yellow toothed grin and gives an enthusiastic "thumbs up" before disappearing into the bushes along the road. People are always interested in my bike. They like the look and are curious about the lifestyle. Offering a friendly response, I'm bombarded with questions. By looking radical and acting moderate, I'm educating people, making them realize that first impressions are often wrong, hoping to squelch a few of their prejudices.

I spend the night in Worland, Wyoming with Cam Henrichsen, a high school friend. He works for the Bureau of Land Management, managing about 300,000 acres of desert badlands, complete with cows and wild horses. Living here has turned him into quite a cowboy, his hat, his horse, his truck, and his six-shooters are now his best friends. Our lives have taken different paths but we still agree on our basic philosophies, freedom and the pursuit of cold beer. A cowboy and a biker aren't really much different. He talks me into staying for the day.

June 29, Worland, Wyoming

Cam has to work for a little while this morning. Waiting for him, I go into town and lube my throttle, wash my bike, and lots of other little things that it thanks me for. I'm sitting on Main Street when a bent old man hobbles up on a cane.

"Nice machine, good to see young folks taking care of their rides."

"Thanks."

"Where ya headed?"

"Alaska, coming from Houston, Texas." I live 100 miles north of Houston but nobody knows where Trinity is.

"Alaska's a good place to see. I can tell that you know what's important. My kids think I'm crazy, but I know what's important too. If I could, I'd say to hell with them and jump on that bike and go with you!"

I thought about offering him a ride but he could barely walk so I decided against it. When old, I am going to say to hell with everybody and do whatever I want, no matter how uncouth. I'll be sitting with my family at Thanksgiving dinner with a fat cigar in my mouth telling dirty jokes, laughing some obnoxious laugh. They will have to look at me and say, "Don't mind him, that's just Grandpa and he's gotten a little crazy the past few years." Either that or they will put me in a rest home where I can make passes at all the nurses. You can get away with a lot if people think you are senile.

After lunch Cam takes me out into the desert on horseback. We spend almost an hour getting the horses prepared for the ride. Cam has always been a bit on the obsessive side. When he starts taking equipment out of his truck it is obvious that each piece is folded and stored in a particular way. It is also expected that I will handle each item accordingly. Little is said but much is understood. I can tell that I am being tested to see if I can remember the things about horses that I learned back in Dakota. I am sure he wonders if I have become "urbanized" and forgotten. Each piece of tack has to be fitted and placed exactly right on the horse. This is for the horse's comfort and safety. I am doing fine until I screw up putting on the breast collar.

Cam notices out of the corner of his eye, almost instinctively, and quickly corrects me.

I am riding Cam's old reliable steed, a horse that knows what to do and requires little skill to ride. Cam is riding a recently acquired wild horse. He got the horse through the federal Adopt-A-Horse program. It was greenbroke at a Wyoming prison and now the rest is up to him. Wild horses are actually feral, domesticated animals that have escaped and thrived in the wild. The original wild horses were descendants of horses lost by the Spanish Conquistadors hundreds of years ago. They were small sleek animals that adapted well to the American deserts. During the early part of this century the stock was mixed with a variety of other breeds. This was due to the invention of automobiles and mechanized farm equipment. The decline of farms and ranches during the Depression also contributed. People who no longer needed their horses or could not afford to care for them often simply let them go rather than selling them or having them destroyed. The current stock of wild horses has a distinctive appearance, mostly due to mixing with large draft horses. Cam's horse is not a large animal , it's actually quite slim around the chest, but it has huge feet and hooves. This, in addition to its round sloping nose, makes it look like some sort of strange medical experiment where parts of different animals were sewn together to create a strange new beast of burden.

The farm where the horses are corralled is right on the edge of the desert, federal land managed by the BLM. Without fear of trespassing we head aimlessly out into the rocky terrain, letting the horses choose their own path. Cam is using a squeaky, brand new, custom saddle and is worried about the affect this will have on an already skittish horse. I wonder what his horse is thinking, having once roamed this desert wild and free, now under our control and forced to follow our wishes and commands. Is he thinking about throwing Cam and taking off into the desert? "If he decided to go, we would never catch him. That would be the last we would see of him or my new saddle." Maybe the horse enjoys this life, plenty of food and water, and Cam loves horses like no one else I know.

The horses travel over steep slopes and through washed out gullies with amazing skill. I simply hold on and trust my ride to choose the best path. The similarities between this and riding my bike are obvious. The differences are a little more subtle. It is more wild and free, traveling off the highway. We can hear nature all around us and can carry a conversation, both impossible on my bike. The relationship between me and the horse is different. I try but I can't completely trust him. Each time we go through some rough terrain I am scared, he can sense it and loses faith in me as his master. He takes over and carries us through, humbling me in the process. It is obvious that I am on a living being with personality, not a machine.

After the hot afternoon in the desert, we head to Goose's Lounge to wash the dust out of out throats and take the sore out of out legs. I take a little too much medicine. The night fades into a hazy blackness in my memory.

June 30, Worland, Wyoming

I leave Worland with only a hangover to remind me of the great time I had throwing darts at Goose's last night. Taking deep breaths of the cool morning breeze, I hold the air in my lungs. It soaks up the alcohol and I blow out, trying to expel the hangover from my body. Each lungfull of fresh air seems to revive me, bringing me closer to sobriety. The air is clean and fresh, like I am the first to ever breath it. Today will be my first day on roads not before traveled; unfamiliar territory.

On I-90 near Livingston, Montana, I take time to look at the people in the cars that pass. The people are always looking back. Walking the sidewalks in any city, people pay less attention to each other than on the freeway. Are we hoping to find the man or woman of our dreams on the highway? Not very likely, but we always look. Maybe it is just practice for the dating game, giving her that "look" without any fear of rejection or sexual harassment lawsuits. But what are you going to do if it works? Sometimes I smile. Sometimes they wave back. One time, riding on the freeway near Denver, a beautiful woman pulled up along side of me. She cast a wonderful smile and gave me an encouraging wave. I missed my exit and had to backtrack about ten miles.

Kids are the best. they think that bikes and trucks are great. Most wave madly as if they are seeing a long lost friend or a movie star. I always wave back. I often see parents scolding their children for their excitement. How many mothers want their kids to grow up to be bikers? I often imagine my mother holding her fragile new bundle to her bosom thinking, "I hope he grows up to be a biker!"

I do believe that most adults want to be bikers, at least for a day. People dress as bikers for parties, most just don't have the guts to do it for real. Women have come up to me saying, "I am trying to talk my husband into getting a bike but he is afraid."

My reply is automatic, "Drop him and get a biker, or better yet, get a bike yourself!" In the end, most people are afraid of true freedom.

"Those who would give up essential
Liberty to purchase a little temporary
Safety, deserve neither Liberty nor Safety.
-Ben Franklin

Before exiting the freeway, I see more personalized license plates than ever before, one group of five in a row. I am beginning to wonder if there is some sort of license plate convention going on. Suddenly a maroon Continental with Minnesota plates pulls up next to me. At first I think the lady is waving but quickly realize that she is pointing at me signaling, "Where's your helmet?" Three kids are standing in the back seat pointing their fingers saying, "Naughty, naughty, naughty!" She must not know that Montana does not have a helmet law, but it does have a child seat belt law. She pulls away and settles back into her 85 mile per hour pace waiting to hurl her grandchildren through the windshield. I follow her, hoping she will stop somewhere, so I can give her a piece of my mind about the unbuckled kids in her back seat, but my exit comes first. She probably still thinks that I am the ignorant one.

After exiting the freeway, I stop in Clyde Park to fuel up and get a drink. At $1.51 per gallon, this is some of the most expensive gas in the U.S.. I walk into the tavern and am greeted by Wal-Mart cowboy decor on blood red walls. I immediately head to the bathroom and am greeted by newly painted signs reading **"Squaws"** and **"Bucks."** Appalled by their bigotry, I piss on the floor and leave without getting a drink.

Driving north from Livingston you really get an idea why they call Montana the "Big Sky Country." The views extend for miles without trees but it's not flat. Rolling hills and ranges of mountains are always in view. The deep blue sky does not end at the horizon; it extends far beyond, making the distant mountains look smaller. The colorless highway is lonesome and the towns that are scattered along the way are almost deserted. All these things together make me feel small. Near Wilsall I see patches of green irrigated fields. From a distance there is no definite shape or pattern to these areas. They look like the greens for a giant golf course.

Along Highway 89 I see some of the dumpiest towns in the U.S.. Most are deserted cattle towns but some, higher up in the mountains, appear to be mining towns. Passing Ringling on the left I see a beautiful church falling apart on a hill to the right. It proudly rests upon a bed of unkept grass and shrubs. The paint has been weathered away and shingles are missing, exposing the rafters below, like the ribs peering out of a decaying corpse. The remains of a few stained glass windows sit loosely in their frames. In too much of a hurry to stop, I fail to hear the stories this building is dying to tell me.

As the day nears its end, I pass through the little mining town of Neihart, nestled in the Little Belt Mountains. This village has no modern buildings. Most are sagging from years of neglect. The sun has long ago washed the colors from their sides. It appears as if the road is squeezing them into the walls of the canyon or rather the walls of the canyon are pushing them into the road where they will be smashed into oblivion by the speeding trucks that pass through. One way or another the highway will destroy this town.

I camp in a forest service campground just outside of town. It is too close to the road and is unkept. Too tired to go on, I don't pay my camping fee in protest of their neglect. Crossing the highway to cool my feet in a nearby stream, I come upon a small deer. I have not alerted the young buck to my presence, so I sit and watch him eat while the songs of the birds change from day to evening.

July 1, Neihart, Montana

It is a cool ride into Great Falls, where I plan to get some transmission lube. The shop is not open when I pull in, so I sit and wait. About 45 minutes later, employees start arriving. They open the door, but are not ready for business for another half an hour. The two quarts of tranny lube cost $5.95 each. It takes a quart and about a quarter cup to fill a Sportster transmission. It will cost me over $12 to change my fluid, wasting almost a whole quart. I voice my complaint about this waste and the price. The blond working the counter responds, "Why are you complaining? You can't go anywhere else!"

I go out back and drain my fluid but decide to mix a little of the old with the new and return a quart. The blond is gone and a different guy is working the till. He starts giving me my money back when I here a voice from a back office yell, "We don't do refunds on oil."

"Are you serious? I haven't even left the shop."

"Yes! I'm serious, we don't do refunds on oil."

"Screw it!" I throw the unopened jug of oil away as I walk out the door mumbling, "Don't you guys think about digging this out of here."

Just before I pull away, the guy at the till comes out with six bucks in his hand and quietly gives it to me.

The Rocky Mountains form a foreboding wall to the west. A dirt track cuts into a neon yellow field of sweet clover. The two dusty ribbons dissappear in the distance, but seem to run straight into the mountains. Above the mountains, hover strange looking lenticular clouds. Formed by strong winds from the mountains, these clouds are sometimes mistaken for flying saucers. They form an evenly spaced line of perfectly formed ovals parallel to the mountains. I take this as a sign of a change in the weather. Since it has been warm and sunny, it is not a welcome sign.

The stretch of dumpy Montana towns ends with Browning. Browning is the roughest, dirtiest place I have seen; a real Old West town. On the edge of the Blackfoot reservation, it is occupied by Indians and cowboys. Not Texas cowboys with starched jeans and perfect George Straight hats, but real cowboys with shit on their boots, holes in their pants, and sweat stained hats. The town is busy, in fact crazy. Cars are backed up everywhere. I stop to mail some cards at the post office and have to wait in line. Kids are tearing up the roads in 4x4s and dirt bikes. I am almost expecting to see somebody riding through on a horse with pistols blazing in the air. I wonder about it all, until I realize that it is the first of the month, government payday for the Indians. I gas up and get out of Dodge, or rather Browning.

Heading up into Glacier National Park, the transition from desert prairie to mountain is very gradual. The burnt grass slowly gets greener and scattered aspen and birch start to appear until they dominate the landscape. Soon, they too give way to pines and firs. Before I expect it, the mountaintops rise above the treeline. Not 14,000 feet like Colorado, but peaks less than 10,000 feet. For some reason they seem more impressive than Colorado. The peaks and ridges are more rugged and unrefined, each with its own personality. In Colorado, the mountains may be stronger and more healthy, but in their youth they have not yet developed their own personality. They all look pretty much the same. "Going to the Sun Highway" peaks in the park at Logan Pass, 6,646 feet. I stop for a quick hike and end up going a couple miles back. I keep thinking the top must be just a little farther. I finally make it. The view is incredible. I am surrounded by snow with little lakes looking out to the sky. Mountain goats share the trail with me. Uninterested in my presence, they simply step off the trail until I pass and then continue their wandering.

On the way back down the other side of the park I notice a change in the weather. Dark clouds are looming in the west and north. I stop in Whitefish to stock up on groceries, trying to ignore the possibility of rain. I proceed toward the Canadian border looking for a campsite. All are full—Fourth of July weekend. The long day is taking its toll on me. My arms feel like they are becoming part of my handlebars, my neck is stiff, and I can't feel my bottom. I rock back and forth in my seat to try and get some blood flowing through my aching butt. I finally pull up alongside a family in a pick-up camper and ask if they mind if I camp nearby. They agree without appearing hospitable.

July 2, Eureka, Montana

I pack my tent wet for the first time, but definitely not the last. I am excited about crossing into British Columbia, but also a little apprehensive. The magnitude of the trip is hitting me. I have been on the road ten days and am just now crossing into Canada. The reality of cold and rain is upon me. For a few minutes it looks like it is going to clear off, but no such luck. At first it doesn't seem to be raining enough to put on my rainsuit, but soon my leathers are wet and slimy. The collar on my jacket is sticky and chafing my neck. I have to force myself to turn my head to check the blind spot when passing. When I do turn, it bites my neck and sends a blast of cold air into a newly exposed opening around my neck. I begin to wonder if I am really prepared for this. 'It could be cold and wet the whole time, will I be able to take it? What if I break down or worse, get hurt?' I could stop here and explore the Rockies, close to home. Nobody would have to know.

I am also starting to worry about money. I have less than a thousand dollars to spend on this entire trip. A major breakdown or unexpected expense could leave me stranded and broke. I have heard horror stories about the prices in Canada and Alaska. I have considered the possibility of taking a seasonal cannery job while I am in Alaska, but I would prefer to leave that task to wandering college students. Money will always be on my mind, but I remind myself that this is part of the challenge.

"A tight budget is the mother of adventure."
-Tim Cahill

Adding to my apprehension is the fact that I am in bear country now. I have never camped around bears, but there have been plenty of people to remind me of them. The same morbid way that people like to remind me that riding a bike is dangerous. Strangers will come up, saying, "My son was killed on a bike." What do they want me to say? Do they want sympathy or reassurance? "I'm sorry" or "He died happy." Some share all the gory details thinking that they might save

35

me. Some show through their glares that they blame me for their loss. Nobody has ever come up to me in my pickup and said, "My son was killed in a pickup." People assume that auto fatalities are the fault of the driver or just an accident, yet the motorcycle is to blame for bike fatalities.

Crossing the border into Canada, my nervous feelings intensify, like I have done something wrong and am about to be busted. I always get this feeling at border crossings. It is the way the guards treat you—like you are guilty and need to prove your innocence. I am asked about my criminal record. A drunk driving conviction, many years ago makes me an undesirable immigrant. I could probably get into Canada but it would cost a processing fee; a couple hundred dollars according to Mark. Instead of paying the money I lie, telling them my record consists of only a couple speeding tickets. They are also convinced that I have a gun.

"Where do you hide your pistol?"

"Don't have one."

"What kind of bear gun do you carry?"

"I don't."

He persists, "Most bikers have guns, do you realize that when I search your bike and find it I will confiscate both the gun and your bike?"

By this time I wished that I had a gun to give him so I could go on. Finally, he is convinced.

When I tell him that I am a teacher in Texas he eyes me with suspicion and asks for proof. What proof do I have? Finally, I find my insurance card and he lets me through.

Canada is different enough to make you feel like you are in another country yet similar enough to make you feel comfortable. Signs are labeled in kilometers instead of miles. I tape a conversion chart to my speedometer and almost wreck a couple times trying to figure out how fast I should be going. People speak English yet most hold on to the accent of their ancestors whether it is French or English or something else. Almost all of them say "Eh?" a lot. "Crappy weather we're having, eh?"

36

The mountains have mellowed into rolling hills, yet the columnar evergreen trees persist. I will ride among this spruce forest for the rest of my journey. It extends almost all they way to the Arctic Circle. It will become a welcome friend.

Not long after crossing the border, I stop to put on my rainsuit at a pullout overlooking Columbia Lake. Another biker on a Suzuki Intruder is drinking coffee, watching me suit up. He is wearing a red rainsuit and sports a very full graying mustache. His short stout body adds to his overall appearance that would make him an excellent candidate to become a Santa Clause in a few years. Joe offers me some coffee and I gladly accept. He has doctored the whole thermos with cream and sugar; I always drink my coffee black, but this cup sells me on the taste of these extras. I find out that he is an artist from Edmonton and is enjoying newfound freedom as a recent divorcee.

We ride together to Invermere where I exchange money and get some lunch. I get $1.37 exchange for my American dollars. While we are eating a guy on a fat Harley Heritage Softail pulls up and joins us. Ben is also from Edmonton where he flies for the Canadian Air Force. He has dark features and a distinctive French nose to compliment his accent. His helmet is a perfectly round bowl with yellow reflectors encircling the brim. He looks like a UFO has landed on his head, "It is really light, an old Ski-Doo snow machine helmet, the cops don't seem to have any problems with it." An oversized pair of aviator goggles complete his comic appearance. We ride through the rain and cold together to Banff. On the way we stop at a rest area, Joe goes in first and comes out saying, "Don't go in there Ben; I don't think they like Frenchmen."

The graffiti exclaims, "Put all frogs in graves." I find out that Canada has its share of political problems. It is interesting to hear politics and problems in another country. I learn all about the Canadian controversy of recruiting immigration versus maintaining cultural identity and the problems between the British and the French, each wanting autonomy. Joe and Ben are the perfect pair to explain the issue, Joe McGoldrick being as much British as Ben Massicotte is French.

Bartell

> "To agree to disagree, to harness diversity,
> to respect dissent; perhaps this is the real
> essence of Canada."
> > -Robert Perry.

We have coffee with the elk that wander the streets of Banff. Banff is a tourist town set amongst the most fantastic scenery I have ever seen. The surrounding mountains look like they have been pushed and heaved into all kinds of uncomfortable positions. Overlooking the city is a ridge that rises conservatively on one side, then suddenly falls drastically into the valley below as if a huge knife carved half of it off and tossed it carelessly to the other side. As we get ready to ride, we say good-bye to Joe. He is getting a room here. Ben and I are camping out. Joe pulls out then whips around the block, "Hell, you guys can share my room, no charge." We accept.

After warming up and drying off, I call Stacy, a friend in Alaska. She renews my excitment for the trip and assures me of the great experiences I am about to encounter. "Isn't Banff great? Alaska is a hundred times better and no people!" I get off the phone, no longer depressed, ready to roll.

We go to a pub for dinner. Prime rib with fixins for $7.95. Considering the exchange rate this is a cheap meal. Meals are reasonable throughout Canada, but gas is a different story. As high as 70 cents a litre or about $1.80 a gallon. During the conversation at the pub we find out that Joe was in the band that recorded the "Rodeo Song." An American/Canadian classic!

> "It's forty below but I don't give a fuck,
> got a heater in my truck,
> and it's off to the rodeo......"
> "Piss me off, fuckin' jerks, get on my nerves."

July 3, Banff, Alberta

The weather looks good pulling out of Banff, but it soon turns to more cold drizzle. The scenery here is incredible, possibly some of the most beautiful mountains anywhere lightly dusted with last night's snow—but they are obscured by clouds. The fact that the tops of the peaks disappear in the weather makes them seem more mysterious and supernatural. The rivers are shades of turquoise blue, a characteristic of glaciation. It adds to the mystique of the place. I have a feeling of awe the whole time I am here.

The parkway follows the valley giving excellent views of the surrounding scenery above. Many of the park roads in the U.S. take you to the tops of the mountains, conquering them, making you look down on them. Here the road slides meekly through the valley allowing you to look up to the mountains. *They* look down on us, as they should. In the shadow of a mountain, the greatest man is nothing.

Joe and Ben peel off at Saskatchewan River Crossing heading back to Edmonton, I continue north toward Jasper. Halfway between Banff and Jasper the Icefields Parkway hits its highest point and I hit a little snow. Soon the Athabasca Glacier reveals itself and greets me with a blast of icy air. Waters from this mass of ice drain into the Atlantic, the Pacific, and the Arctic Oceans. Having never before seen a glacier, I am amazed. On a glacier you can see, feel, and hear one of the forces that shapes our planet. The ice is melting, the sound of running water can be heard everywhere. The ice appears to be solid, but it is moving. Occasional moans, groans, and booms are testimony. Piles of rocks and debris are the evidence. Once I am on the glacier, deep cobalt blue crevasses reveal themselves. Some could be hundreds of feet deep, but most appear to be relatively shallow. Many smaller glaciers hang from the steep sides of the valley like broken waterfalls. I will see many more glaciers before the end of my trip, but will never tire of them.

After walking on the glacier, I take a break in the visitor center to warm up. The place is packed with tourists. I thought I had escaped the Fourth of July crowds by leaving the US, but I figure out that this weekend is also Victoria Day in Canada. Interestingly, the crowds are not just Canadians enjoying the weekend, but Asians actually dominate the crowd. Stereotypical Asians, each with about four cameras and camcorders hanging from their necks. They have come on package bus trips. When they arrive someplace, they take it over. Then suddenly they are gone and the place is deserted, until the next bus arrives.

I retreat the restroom where I sit under the hand dryer—trying to warm up. The hot air actually feels like it is burning my hands. Soon I am warmed up and ready to hit the road. As soon as I step outside I realize that the dryer wasn't the best idea. It now seems twenty degrees colder out here. I can hardly force myself to get back on my icy cold bike and hit the wind.

I make it another hundred miles to Tete Jaune Cache and set up camp. The name means 'the White man's hiding place', or literally, 'Yellow Hair's hiding place.' The local campground has been destroyed by a mudslide, but the owners of a motel let me camp behind their house. I build a small fire to warm up and am soon joined by the teenage son of the motel owners. He quizzes me about my trip and my lifestyle. I can see a look of amazement in his eyes. Trying to impress me he tells of a grizzly that has been sighted nearby.

"We went out there yesterday to try to find it, but didn't see anything. Don't tell my dad, he would kill me if he found out we were up on the mountain looking for a bear. We told him we were fishing."

Now I'm thinking about bears! I ask him to take my food inside with him to keep them out of camp.

Before I go to sleep, I notice his teenage sisters staring at me through their bedroom windows. I wonder what kind of life they live when a single biker can arouse such curiosity.

July 4, Tete Jaune Cache, British Columbia

I wake to more rain, and pack my tent wet. The owners of the motel invite me inside for coffee. They take this opportunity to try to save my soul, fundamental Christians. We discuss all kinds of things from creationism to the infallibility of the bible. I consider being baptized right on the spot to make them feel better about my soul. Instead I sit quietly until I am warm and politely leave them to their beliefs.

With a dense covering of forest and few side roads this stretch of Highway 16 to Prince George feels truly remote. I meet very few cars and see abundant of wildlife, numerous deer but no bears. The four "towns" along this 180 mile stretch of highway are hardly more than a gas station and cafe. Most have their own generators, no power lines. I truly get the feeling, for the first time that I am driving through wilderness.

The near freezing rain is a fine mist that makes my face tingle and ache with its indefinite stings. Several stretches of construction keep me on my toes and coat me with chalky mud. At Prince George the road turns north toward Dawson Creek and the beginning of the Alaskan Highway. Judging by my pace I will make it tonight with ease. An hour north of Prince George, near McLeod Lake, the sun comes out. I stop along the road to dance and holler in the warmth. I will make it to Dawson Creek with plenty of time to spare.

About another hour down the road, I stop to take in a waterfall and am greeted by two guys in a beat up Datsun 210. Chris and Bob are both short and stout, but not fat. They speak with a musical high-pitched accent that reminds me of the munchkins from *The Wizard of Oz*. They work construction in Chetwynd. "Why don't you follow us to town? We'll buy a beer for a fellow rider and you won't believe what the dancers do with a 'looney'." A looney is a Canadian dollar coin with a loon on the back. They have my interest.

We pull into Chetwynd, the chainsaw capitol of the world. Several chainsaw sculptures guard the entrance sign. The town has little of interest, a couple of hotels and gas stations and plenty of trailer houses. Maybe it should be the trailer house capitol of the world. I am sure some Southern U.S. town already has that distinction.

I follow the Datsun to a hotel bar with a muddy gravel parking lot full of pick-up trucks. As my eyes adjust to the dark room I see bare walls and a concrete floor covering an area half as big as a basketball court. If the walls were not painted stark white, I don't think it would be possible to see at all. There are no two matching tables or chairs. The bar is plywood with four old refrigerators and a couple of neon lights. Along one wall is a plywood stage, about two feet off the floor. Most of the tables are occupied by either Indians or construction workers who have not bothered to change; Carhart brand jeans and rubber boots are the standard attire.

I hear my name and see that my hosts have already found a table, next to the stage. As soon as I take off my jacket and sit down, an Indian comes over, stands in front of me, and looks me in the eye. He says nothing, just reaches down, grabs a handful of my beard and jerks my head back and forth three times.

Chris and Bob jump up yelling, "Kick his ass, Kick his fuckin' ass!!"

I grab his hand, thinking, "I'm 2,000 miles away from home, out of my country and nobody knows where I am. The last thing I need is to get into a fight with somebody who probably has about 50 relatives in here."

I look at him, still gripping his hand, "What the FUCK are you trying to do?"

He gets a stupid look on his face and says, "You're not George!"

"You're god-dammed fucking right I'm not George, get the fuck away from me!"

The poor guy spends the next hour apologizing to us and buying us rounds. I'm still not sure if he really thought I was somebody else or maybe got scared when he saw that I wasn't alone. Before leaving, I see three good fights, and one guy gets stoned. I mean stoned in the biblical context, they threw him out of the bar and threw fist sized rocks at him to drive him away.

Soon the first dancer comes on stage. She is not at all unsightly. The short blond hardly looks old enough to be dancing. She does the usual cabaret stuff with a casual indifference that appears to separate her from what she is doing. After she gets rid of all of her clothes she puts her feet behind her head. She then takes a looney, licks it, and puts it on her neatly trimmed privates. "If any of you boys can knock this off you get a blow-job!"

After a few minutes I slide up to the stage and toss a couple coins. Humored by my cheesy grin, several people bring their own coins for me to throw. I end up with a pile, throwing one after another but none hit their target. Hundreds of loonies are thrown but nobody knocks it off. Many come close, hitting the coin, jiggling it like it was glued to rubber, but it holds, almost magically. The better the hit the more she coos and moans, encouraging suckers to throw more. Rumor has it that a blow-job is a type of drink. I'll never know for sure.

Before long I am offered a sleeping spot in a warehouse leased by my hosts. I ask why they have a warehouse. They tell me they have a little business on the side and give me a sly wink. Without much calculation I figure that I do not want to be proximal to whatever their business might be. Before I have too many beers to drive, I make up an excuse about needing to be in Dawson Creek bright and early. Tactfully, I make my escape.

Joe McGoldrick and Ben Masscotte in Banff National Park.

Lycrecia Put me up for the night, Fort Nelson, BC.

A stoic pose in Stone Mountain Provincial Park, BC.

Chris, my German companion, Stone Mountain Provincial Park.

Harley's Northernmost Outpost, Fairbanks, AK.

Skinny Dick's Halfway Inn, Get it?

With Clint Seyer, First Alaskan State HOG Rally, Anchorage.

With Bert at the Bird House Bar.
The camera is level, the bar is sloping.

"Can I have my picture taken with you?" Valdez.

From the air the movement of a glacier is apparent.

July 5, Dawson Creek, British Columbia

I camp at a city park and then spend the morning washing myself, my laundry, and my bike. I want to start the Alcan fresh and clean. Dawson Creek lies on the edge of the spruce forest that sprawls all the way to the Pacific. Traveling east of here, you are greeted by a patchwork of flourishing fields of grain. The town's highlights are an art gallery in a red grain elevator and "Mile 0" of the Alaskan Highway. This "Midwestern" town is not at all what I expected at the beginning of the Alcan. I have a delicious lunch at the Alaskan Hotel, noted for unusual dishes, stir fry with cantaloupe and honeydew.

While waiting my turn to take pictures of "Mile 0" I overhear a couple of guys talking about bad construction on the highway.

"It's near Beaver Creek, just before the Alaskan border, 120 miles of foot deep mud and ruts. People are going off the road and getting stuck everywhere." Hardly encouraging news, but I chalk it up as merely exaggerated gossip.

I am definitely not the first to attempt this trip on a bike. The first attempt was made by a fellow named Slim Williams. Slim was a proponent of the Alaskan highway and 1933 he mushed a team of sled dogs from Fairbanks to Chicago for the World's Fair. He hoped the publicity would build support for a highway connecting Alaska to the Lower Forty-eight. In 1939 he conjured up another stunt—a ride through the wilderness on motorcycles. The trip, from Fairbanks to Seattle, took him and his partner over six months. They covered 2,200 miles, often blazing their own trail and using canvas rafts to cross streams.

I leave Dawson Creek under a sunny sky and a warm breeze. Suddenly, it clouds up and the temperature drops. The road is excellent—smooth with wide shoulders, much different than the trail slim had to face. It sits high in the landscape, offering extended views of the surrounding wilderness that expands in all directions. I see my first bear popping out of the woods and then quickly disappearing again, "Oops, I didn't want to stick my head out here!"

At Bucking Horse River some soup and coffee warms me up. While I sit shivering, a woman comes in and studies me. She is a

Native with cropped hair, a pierced nose, and Converse Chuck Taylor sneakers. Not your normal Northern Canadian garb. She gets a pen and paper from the counter and comes over. "If you need a shower or anything when you get to Fort Nelson give me a call. My name is Lycrecia." She hands me her number. About fifty miles outside of Fort Nelson it starts to pour; I can barely see the road. Soon, my rainpants split open at the crotch; by the time I reach town I am soaked from the inside out. Bordering on hypothermia, I stop to gas up and call Lycrecia. She shares a trailer with her sister and offers me her nephew's bed for the evening. The sun sets all night. Before falling asleep, I see a rainbow outside my window; it is almost midnight.

July 6, Fort Nelson, BC

Lycrecia cooks me breakfast in the morning. After we eat she takes me on a tour of the Slave (slay-vee) reservation. This is a very new reservation, established in 1959. Prior to the move, most of the tribe lived on the river near the Old Fort. As late as 1969, some were still resisting the move and lamenting over their loss (the soil here is not nearly as fertile as that along the river bottom.)

Lycrecia is too young to remember anything but the reserve. She seems proud of the development in the small area they have been given. "One family is going to build a gas station and convenience store. They are striving to be self sufficient."

She takes me to her parents' house, they are more traditional than she and speak a mixture of English and their native tongue. I never see them, they speak through a closed bedroom door. The house smells of smoked fish and buckskin. The buckskin is braintanned the traditional way. The hides are dehaired and scraped to remove all the epidermis and then soaked in a solution of mashed brains and water. Supposedly, each animal has enough brains to tan its own hide. After the hide is soaked in the solution it is worked over a board or a rope. The stretching and pulling continues to soften the hide until it is completely dry. The hide is then smoked to give it a golden brown color and waterproof it. The finished product is one of the softest materials I have ever felt. Several unfinished leather bags and garments are lying around. Hanging on the wall are a pair of moccasins and mukluks—the traditional winter footwear of Northern natives.

We go into the garage and she reveals a pink Sportster. She is planning a ride to Utah in a couple of weeks, an impressive trip for a single woman. Actually, an impressive trip for anybody. I give her a few suggestions to deal with the heat. Before I leave, she gives me some smoked moose meat for my saddle bags.

A couple of hours out of Fort Nelson the road narrows and presents some of the best topography of the entire stretch. I take several breaks, waiting for trains of slower vehicles to pass. This allows me to race up the hills and through the curves uninhibited. I especially enjoy a couple a banked curves at the bottom of steep grades. I pick up speed going down and lean into the curve as it hits bottom. The g-forces squeeze me into my seat. I am enjoying this roller coaster ride until I misjudge one curve. I go in a little fast and it has no bank. I panic and tighten up, heading for the ditch. Instinctively I relax and lean into the curve and make it. I pause to let my pounding heart settle down before continuing. I should know better than to take unnecessary risks here, hours away from medical attention.

I see lots of wildlife along the highway including about a dozen bears, one sow with cubs playing in the ditch. I stop to take a picture of one of the bears wondering what would happen if he decides to attack. I'd be sitting here with my hands full of camera trying to ride away. I'd probably wipe out and get eaten. Not a bad way to go. It would give the folks back home something to talk about for years.

While I'm taking the picture, a guy on a Kawasaki dirt bike pulls up and snaps one too. He follows me through Stone Mountain Provincial Park where we see caribou and stone sheep living among rocky peaks. Stone Mountain is an appropriate name for this park. The mountains hold little vegetation. It is as if they are just now reaching puberty and starting to grow their adult hair. One sawtooth ridge is so geometrical that the peaks appear to be huge pyramids with perfect alluvial fans flowing from between them.

My shadow rider is a German named Chris. His KL 650 is loaded beyond belief. A high tank bag in front and a huge pack in back leave almost no room for him to squeeze into the seat between. The top heavy bike threatens to flip over each time he perches it on its stand. He wears a full suit of leathers color coordinated with his helmet. He has a long straggly beard and a balding head. Antique wire glasses sit loosely on his hollow face. Without his gear he would look more like a monk than a biker. He speaks very little English, so our conversation is limited since I speak no German. Nevertheless, he follows me for three days.

We stop at Toad river to fuel up and eat lunch. While at the pump an airplane lands on the highway, pulls in, and fuels up next to me! Tired from the rough ride, I toss my jacket carelessly on the ground and lie on it with my cheese and crackers spread out in front. I eat, leaning against my bike, stretching my legs out. Some movement catches my eye, I spin around just in time to see a bear run past about thirty feet behind us. Soon every stupid tourist with a camera follows its path trying to get a shot or maybe trying to get eaten. The owner of the roadhouse comes running out with his rifle. After a few minutes we hear a shot out in the bush. This bear had been stealing garbage for a couple of weeks. Soon they lose their fear of humans and that makes them dangerous. A fed bear is a dead bear!

Fuel is not a problem along the Alcan, about every fifty or sixty miles there is a roadhouse with gas pumps, a tow truck, a restaurant, and sometimes a motel and a campground. There are no power lines here, they have their own generators. Each establishment is unique and relies on the tourists for its livelihood. During the winter they get more peace and quiet than we can imagine, they must like it that way.

We stop by Muncho Lake for a few photos. The teal blue colors of this long narrow lake can not be captured on film. This color is due to leaching from the copper rich mountainsides rather than from glacial silt like most other bodies of water in the region. Muncho is a native word meaning, "big deep water." Mountains surround the water like a huge hand made bowl. The highway is carved into the side of these mountains that threaten to push us into the sharp dropoff that dissappears into the cold waters of the lake.

The road has turned bad, loose gravel and huge potholes abound. In theory, the Alcan is now a paved road, but the word "pavement" is applied loosely here. The surface, in most sections, is simply a layer of gravel, sprayed with oil and covered with crushed rock.. Over time the traffic packs the rock into the oil soaked gravel creating "pavement." I can take the heel of my boot and without much effort dig a hole in it.

We find out that this section of the highway had been resurfaced just two days earlier. The contractor mixed the oil wrong and it rained. The oil and water mixed, creating a sticky mess of tar. As people drove over it, huge chunks of the highway stuck to their tires, creating the potholes and coating their vehicles with tar. We see the effects in the ditch, a camper trailer with a broken axle and later, a bike with a bent rim. The guy is trying to get the tire to seal by pounding on the bend with a couple of rocks. We offer our assistance, but he declines. A couple of guys on Harleys with belt drives blew belts and ruined their sprockets. They were still in Whitehorse trying to get going when we got there.

Chris and I stop at Liard Hot Springs for a swim. The water is almost too hot to bear, it feels like heaven around my sore body. The geothermal springs heat several acres and create an oasis of temperate plants surrounded by the tundra. Early explorers reported the area as a jungle full of ferns, flowers, and even dinosaurs. It definitely could be the site for a cheesy "Land of the Lost" type film.

Not long after hitting the road we come to a pullout called "Allen's Lookout." I am forced to turn around to view the landmark that bears my name. The knoll was an outlook for outlaws who waited here to attack riverboats traveling up the Liard River. From this vantage point, we have a clear view of the gray stream below. A recent fire has killed all the surrounding trees. This, in combination with some dark but dry clouds, gives the whole scene a dreary black and white appearance. A gust of dirty wind commands us to move on.

We ride a couple more hours before agreeing on a campsite alongside a manmade fishing pond. Cooking dinner, Chris is plagued by mosquitoes. None bother me, so I laugh quietly as he puts on a headnet to preserve his sanity. Nowhere in Canada or Alaska do I see the infamous hordes of biting insects that everyone warned me about. I would like to compare them to the terrible concentrations I have seen coming out of the saltwater marshes along the Gulf of Mexico in Texas. Some so bad that campgrounds have to be closed down. Nothing here compares to that.

July 7, Iron Creek, BC

Before we head out I take a walk around the small reservoir that borders our campsite. There are multitudes of lean identical evergreens here sitting in the quaggy ground. A variety of mosses and lichens cushion my feet as I walk the forest floor. As on the tundra in Wyoming, most plants are dwarfed. I see miniature varieties of dogwoods, wild roses, yarrow, and lupines.

Not long after departing we cross into the Yukon. My mind is filled with images from *Call of the Wild*. Ever since I was a child I have always considered the Yukon a mystical wild place. Just the name evokes emotion. "Yukon," an Indian word meaning, "greatest." I am finally here. Stopping at the border to take pictures of the signs, I start to read the graffiti. The most conspicuous reads, "I just love this part of Texas." I can never completely get away from some Texans' arrogance. The road crosses back and forth over the border between British Columbia and the Yukon several times. No signs note which we are in. The highway doesn't care.

We stop for a couple of hours in Watson Lake, the only thing resembling a town we have seen since we left Fort Nelson two days ago. Watson Lake is the first town in the Yukon and is an Alaskan Highway tourist trap hosting musicals and museums about the highway. It was incorporated in 1984. None of the buildings show any age.

Not far from the city is Contact Creek, the spot where the northern and southern road construction crews met in September, 1942 to complete the southern sector of the Alcan. The Alcan was built during WWII to connect Alaska to the Lower Forty-eight. The Canadians furnished the right-of-way in exchange for ownership of the highway after the war. 10,000 men completed the 1,422 mile road in just six months—no small feat.

During the construction of the highway, a U.S. soldier from Danville, Illinois started a signpost forest by putting up a sign from his hometown. Travelers are still adding signs to the 20,000 that now exist. Sign covered posts, over twelve feet high, cover an area larger than a football field. People have put up city limit signs along with other actual road signs. Others, without the foresight to steal a sign for their trip, have fashioned signs out a variety of objects: paper plates, TV trays, hubcaps, and just about anything else you can imagine. A local profiteer has set up a stand selling "professionally" painted signs. People are milling around, looking for a sign from their hometown, or one put up by an acquaintance. I see one couple looking for a sign they put up on a trip ten years ago. A man is walking around with a crowbar, pulling down faded and unreadable signs. I retrieve one from his pile and carve a Harley logo and my hometown in Texas. Chris is excited after finding several signs from Germany, one from his hometown.

In the parking lot, I survey the variety of vehicles that are traveling the highway. By far, he most common is the motorhome. Thousands of elderly couples are traveling the highway, struggling to enjoy their retirement. Overhearing their conversations, I can sense tension in most of their voices. "Take a picture (to prove we were here) and lets get moving again." One night, camping along the road, a huge RV parked beside me. Automatic levels came out, a satellite dish popped up, and I heard the generator kick in. The next morning they pulled out without ever getting out of their vehicle. For all I know there might not have been anybody inside. Maybe it was just a machine.

There is an interesting variety of people who are obviously moving to the North Country. Their cars are packed with all of their belongings, pulling trailers packed beyond capacity. I get the idea that most are trying to escape; looking for something different. They are meeting people who are obviously moving south probably disillusioned with the "adventurous" life in the North or possibly unable to handle the cold dark winters.

Others, like myself, are obviously traveling; looking for an adventure on the highway. A variety of motorcycles, airplanes, four-wheel drives, and classic cars, we despise the RVs for making our trip look casual. Our vehicles have modifications that show that we are seeking adversity: extra gas cans, spare tires, or rock screens over our headlights. I can't help but think of Thurbor's *Walter Mitty,* but with most of the highway paved and fuel every sixty miles, it is not the muddy, dusty adventure that it used to be.

I find the vehicles with Alaska plates the most interesting. They are driving to get somewhere. We are all in their way. This trip is casual. They look like this is a Sunday drive in their family cars and bikes without any extra gear. Very few trucks travel the Alcan. Most choose to take the shorter, but rougher, Cassiar Highway. The Cassiar follows the coast along the panhandle of Alaska without actually connecting to it. It is simply a quick south to north road connecting Prince Rupert (a Canadian port) to Watson Lake and the Alcan.

The Alcan is not a deserted highway, Nevada is a better place to find that. Here there is lots of traffic. You find yourself in a window of travelers. Everywhere you stop you see some of the same people, those who are traveling at about the same speed. You develop a sort of camaraderie with the other travelers. I get the feeling that if something went wrong someone would recognize me and help out. On some stretches of highway in Nevada you could wait several hours for someone to come and help.

As we prepare to leave, a group of riders on Honda GoldWings pulls up. They come over and ask for advice. I am flattered. Two of their bikes have bald tires, one with the cords showing. My advice, "Don't go any farther!" I tell them to have tires shipped from Whitehorse since they would be fools to ride on those tires. They don't want to wait a couple days so they wrap the tires with duct tape and head toward Whitehorse, 300 miles. I hope nobody was hurt. How could someone try a trip like this on bad tires?

For the next three hundred miles to Whitehorse the road is quite nice, interrupted by a few small, muddy sections of construction. I cautiously hold my feet to the side as I slip through the slimy mud. Suddenly my front tire hits a rock and cocks to the side. As I pull it back my bike flails violently to the right. My right foots slaps the ground so hard it hurts all the way up to my hip. I manage to keep my loaded ride upright and continue through, shaken but unharmed.

The topography has mellowed and I am hypnotized by the unchanging landscape. Riding these long sections my butt and legs grow tired. I keep my circulation by moving my feet to a variety of positions on my bike. It has three different sets of foot pegs. I can lean back on my sleeping bag with my feet extended over or upon my

57

forward highway pegs. With my feet on the center control pegs, I can ride with my body upright. Hooking my feet on the rear passenger pegs allows me to lie forward, nearly horizontal, resting on the gas tank. Finally, by combining these positions, I have a variety of awkward ways to alter my riding position and to stretch my legs. Each position makes my bike handle differently and keeps me alert. I sing songs out loud to keep my mind occupied. *Moon Shadow* by Cat Stevens, *Take the Money and Run* by Steve Miller, and *Dead or Alive* by Bon Jovi are some of the songs that I can't get out of my head

I run a soundtrack for this trip over and over in my head. Songs that I have compiled include those over played songs along with a few others: *Hell's Bells* by AC/DC (opening song,) *Midnight Rider* by the Allman Brothers (for a sober mood,) *Lunatic Fringe* by Red Rider, *6 to 9* by Jimmie Hendrix, *The Motorcycle Song* by Arlo Guthrie (for a lighter moment,) and, of course, *Born to Be Wild* by Steppenwolf. I have also added an entire collection of Doors songs.

Late in the afternoon, we set up camp near Whitehorse at Robert Service Campground; motorcycle, bicycle, and walk in camping only. As I get off my bike, my legs are stiff and my butt is sore. After sitting on my bike so long, my coordination on the solid ground is a bit off. I stumble a couple of times while setting up my tent. The park is named after the author of the famous poem, *The Cremation of Sam McGee.*

> "Strange things are done in the midnight sun,
> By the men who moil for gold.
> The Arctic trails have their secret tales,
> That would make your blood run cold.
> The Northern Lights have seen queer sights,
> But the queerest they ever did see,
> Was that night on the marge of Lake LaBarge,
> I cremated Sam McGee."

July 8, Whitehorse, Yukon Territory

Whitehorse was named by the first miners who visited the area and thought that the rapids of the Yukon River resembled the mane of a white horse. The Yukon's source is about a hundred miles south of here, near Skagway and only a few miles from the waters of the Pacific. It flows away from the ocean for hundreds of miles, going through the Yukon and across Alaska before finally emptying into the ocean that it started so near. Whitehorse is near the point where the overland route of Klondike miners from Skagway met the Yukon River. From here the miners had a relatively easy float to Dawson City. Whitehorse became the territorial capitol in 1953 and now holds two-thirds of the 70,000 people who live in the Yukon. It is a modern town with a McDonald's and Kentucky Fried Chicken.

Chris and I will part today, he is going up the "Top of the World Highway" through Dawson City. I am staying on the Alcan. We decide to spend most of the day in town doing tourist things. While riding around I notice a strange knocking noise coming from my engine or perhaps my primary. We stop at the local Harley dealer and ask a mechanic to listen. He nods his head, "Bad gas."

"Are you sure?"

He assures me that most Americans who come through here have troubles with the Canadian fuel. The locals use additives. I'm not convinced, but accept his theory.

At the dealer, I meet some riders from California who are going my way. I decide to spend another night here and ride with them tomorrow. Ken and his wife ride a Honda Gold Wing. Bob and his wife ride Harleys. His is an FLH and her's is a Heritage Softail. Mary is much younger than Bob and is quite beautiful, a contrast to Bob's aged face and white hair. Ken and his wife seem like a typical boring suburban couple on their polished Honda with polyester pants and tacky brown vinyl jackets. I end up enjoying conversation with them more than Bob and Mary. They follow me to the campsite. They have camper trailers complete with every gadget you can imagine, including an electric cooler and Coleman lanterns. As it turns out, I have little in common with these riders. They have bikes, but that is a mere coincidence rather than some sort of commonality.

Camped next to us is a guy in a wheelchair who invites us over for coffee. He lost his legs and one lung in a refinery fire. He now collects 90% disability and is traveling the continent. Clamps hold the firewood he cuts and carpet makes his wheelchair easier to maneuver. He has a perfect setup for camping and relies on nobody except his monthly check and his watchdog. He talks of big adventures, showing little regret and asking for no sympathy.

July 9, Whitehorse, Yukon Territory

We get up early and start our push to Tok, Alaska—400 miles. At Haines Junction the snowcapped Kulane Mountains rise sharply above the surrounding valley. We can feel the cool air falling off the glacier capped peaks. I catch a rare glimpse of a lynx streaking across the road. The scenery gets better and the road gets worse as we progress. The mountains dangerously draw my attention from the narrow road. Frost heaves continually hurl our bikes up and then the road drops out from underneath. My loaded bike is constantly bottoming out, pounding my back. Since day one this highway has been plagued with problems unique to the North country. Building the road caused a scar on the land, thawing the permafrost below. Perfect new sections of highway would fill with water and mud in a couple of days. The army solved this problem by corduroying, putting a blanket of trees under the road to insulate the permafrost. Today the problems continue in the form of frost heaves.

Outside of Destruction Bay we hit about 70 miles of construction, bad construction. This is the infamous Beaver Creek construction, fifty miles shorter than the rumors and today it looks dry. At the first checkpoint a flagperson senses my apprehension, "Don't worry, you'll make it. It's not that bad."

The road is completely torn up and they are putting down a layer of fist sized rocks. Riding on rough gravel it is better to speed up, floating over the bumps and rocks. A bike is like a giant gyroscope; it is made to stay upright while it is moving. The last thing you ever want to do is lock up you brakes—when your wheels stop your gyroscope stops. No more stability. Your bike instantly goes into a violent wobble until you let off the brakes. You don't drive a bike; you ride it. You give it a command, a slight lean or a twist of the throttle, and it knows what it is supposed to do. It will almost always do the right thing. You have to learn to trust it, leaning with it, never fighting it. Once you learn to trust your bike it becomes an extension of your body. You suddenly feel power. Power to move through time and space at whatever rate you want. Riding is so free and pure that I often imagine I'm flying. Reacting without thinking, subconsciously,

61

like I imagine a bird does. They don't think about flying; they just fly. *Slower....Faster....Left.... Right.* It happens. I don't think about riding; I just ride.

Following Mary, I realize that she is having problems handling her bike. Her feet barely reach the ground. She slows down to a crawl. Her "gyroscope" weakens. Each rock sends her veering to one side or the other. She is fighting her bike rather than letting it ride the way it wants to. At irregular intervals huge "Tonka" trucks come roaring by shaking the Earth and throwing a huge cloud of dust. The tires on these monster trucks are at least ten feet high. They are hauling loads of boulders, each as big as a full sized car. Their size makes them appear as though the are just creeping along, but a comparison with my speedometer reveals that they are doing at least fifty miles per hour.

The unsettling presence of these ominous machines is only adding to Mary's problems. At one point her bike rebels, finding a straight path and almost hitting a flagperson. I shake my head in disbelief and apologize to the irate woman who was nearly run over. We make it through, the Californians complaining the whole time. I'm not sure what they expected up here, but they will have to drive it again or else brave 180 miles of washboards and gravel on the road through Dawson City. There are only two ways to drive out of Alaska. Neither is a cinch but I was expecting worse.

Before we cross into Alaska, a water truck pulls out in front of me. He won't let me pass and then dumps water in front of me, presumably to settle dust. I get covered with mud. At the next flagperson, she walks up to me and asks if I got caught behind the water truck. "He likes to dump on bikers, the asshole. I have complained but nobody cares."

Shortly after crossing into Alaska, I have to stop for a bathroom break. After urgently working my way up to the pole position in our caravan, I find a pullout with trash cans but no toilets. I walk out into the bush and relieve myself, gazing into an incredible vista. Mountains reflect off a shimmering marsh. Back at the bikes, Ken points out a sign. "Warning, Rogue Bear!" I wonder if the beast was watching, sizing me up for a meal. Too late to worry about it now.

We make it to Tok, a hundred miles past the border, and agree on a campsite and restaurant after much fretting. Even though the weather is beautiful, Mary wants to get a motel room. Thankfully, none are available. We end up at Rita's RV Park.. Rita is a gruff old lady, revealing a drastic change from the friendly attitudes in Canada. I try to pay for my site with an American Express traveler's check.

"We only take **American** money here." she snips, thinking my check is a Canadian bill. I quickly point out the word "American" on the check. She swallows hard and takes the check.

Setting up camp turns into an ordeal with little conversation. Nobody's tent goes up right. They all just mumble to themselves. With everybody cranky, and no one to talk to, I go to bed early.

July 10, Tok, Alaska

I sleep in and let the Californians leave without me. I am tired of their whining and am ready to travel on my own again. I can now go where I want, when I want without consulting anybody or offending anybody. Finding a good riding partner is a difficult thing. It is harder than finding a good road trip partner in a car. You don't entertain each other and if you get mad you can't deal with it immediately. You ride on letting it boil up inside you until the next stop. You must have similar riding styles and abilities. You must like riding at similar speeds and you must like doing the same types of things. Once you find that, you can just ride and enjoy yourself, no conferences or tiptoeing around. If one wants to stop the other or others will probably enjoy or at least understand the stop. You learn to communicate without talking and work as one on the highway. It is amazing to see a good set of riding partners passing cars like a smooth ripple on a glassy pond.

I go wash my bike and check the primary adjustment. The rattling sound is getting worse. With no other choice I try to make it the 200 miles to Fairbanks.

Stopping for a break near Birch Lake, I take a walk on the bed of a tributary of the Tanana River. With most of the heavy snowmelt over, the river is reduced to a complicated network of small rivulets zigzagging over the wide channel. The bars are composed of a variety of perfectly rounded stones, most as big as my fist. Jumping over several of the small streams, I find a place to sit and listen to the water trickle around. Seeing several large logs tossed onto the banks, I try to imagine what the river would look like during a heavy flow.

The Alaskan Highway officially ends in Delta Junction where I stop to fuel up. When I start my bike back up the rattling is extreme. It sounds like the idling of a cold diesel engine, chugging and clanking. The sound is only when the bike is idling so I pray myself to North Pole, outside Fairbanks. I hear that there is a mechanic nearby, so I go to his house. He agrees that the sound is in my primary. He works at the Harley shop in Fairbanks, "Bring it in tomorrow, we open at 9:00."

I call South Dakota and ask Mark about the primary. "That's bad Allen, I don't know what to tell you." If the shaft is ruined it is bad news, the shaft and flywheels are one piece on a Sportster. Replacement means completely splitting the case and replacing everything. I was worried before, now I'm completely depressed. I sit on the curb, pondering my situation. I can't afford this, but I don't want it to ruin my trip either. I'm here in Alaska, I can't turn back now. Should I buy another bike, a car? No, I need to take care of my immediate needs, a place to pitch my tent and eat dinner.

I find a small city park with free camping and set my tent up next to a Mexican family. They look like they are living here, the trash already accumulating around their tent, their kids taking over the playground. I wonder how long it will be before they are kicked out. Nearby, a hitchhiker repeatedly beats her dog with a stick for no apparent reason. As I walk past her on the way to the toilets, she turns sweet and pleads for money. My response confuses her, "Are you going to beat it out of me, like you beat your dog?" Those who are down always find somebody or something to bring down with them or even put down lower.

> "A dog starved at his master's gate,
> Predicts the ruin of the state."
> -Blake

After eating, I slip into my sleeping bag but can't sleep, my mind is full of my problems. First, I'm depressed and feel like crying, then it changes to disbelief, "this can't be happening now." Soon I'm angry, ready to lash out at somebody or something. Sudddenly, I see the woman beating her dog, but she has my face. This snaps me back to reality. I level out my roller coaster of emotions and go to sleep worried but not angry.

65

July 11, North Pole, Alaska

I wake hoping my problems are just a dream, no such luck. I pack up and get to 'Harley's Northernmost Outpost' an hour before they open. Three other bikes are waiting already. As soon as they open we all go in and fill out service orders. All the others are getting tires and services, I'm the only one with serious problems.

The shop is an attraction in itself, a dilapidated old building with unpainted wooden siding. It is decorated with a conglomeration of antiques, including an outhouse and dog sleds loaded with antlers. While waiting, I see them sell hundreds of dollars worth of T-shirts, mostly to tourists who have heard about the shop. It will soon be a thing of the past. The original owner died and Harley Inc. is pressuring his son to get rid of the old shop or modernize it to fit the new "Harley" image. Another one bites the dust.

I take a walk downtown to kill some time while they look at my bike. The main business area is about seven blocks from the shop. I see nothing unique other than a large number of bars with Indians standing outside. Alcoholism plagues them here just like everywhere else. The bars close for a couple hours every morning, many locals simply stand outside, waiting for them to open again.

I explore several shops and department stores but see very little, my problems continue to consume my thoughts. I am a machine plodding down the aisles, going through the motions of actually shopping. Before long I find myself back at the shop.

While anxiously waiting to find out what my problem is, one of the other customers, a guy on a new FLH, in sneakers and stretch blue jeans, approaches me.

"Why are you here?" he asks.

"My primary on my Sportster is falling apart."

He looks down at me, "No wonder, you have no business taking a Sportster out of town."

I am suddenly on the defensive, "Why are **you** here?"

"Oil change."

"Oil change! Pull your bike over here and I'll change your oil for free."

Nervously he replies, "I'm having warranty work done. M-my throttle is sticking."

I proudly stand up, "If you can't lube your own throttle, you have no business riding any motorcycle!" I walk away from him.

Shortly after this confrontation a large group of bikes, followed by a U-Haul van, pulls into the shop. The van is painted with rugged lettering, **UGLIES MC**. They are an interesting, nation wide club and they are ugly. Full beards and long hair are the norm. A few exceptionally ugly Uglies catch my attention. One is a scrawny, bare chested, old guy with his long beard braided into three, foot long tails. Another balding, red-haired guy, has a full beard with no mustache. He looks like the Cowardly Lion. They began their trip, with their support vehicle, in Colorado. They mill around, some just stretching their legs while others look over their bikes with a purpose. After getting the needed parts, they all pitch in and complete their repairs with more than professional efficiency. All the necessary tools are organized in the back of the van. I see no dissension among the group and all are in high spirits. As the tasks at hand wind down, several begin milling around again. One big dark man comes up to me and asks what I'm writing about in my journal. "You." His face lights up with a warm smile. He reminds me of Grizzly Adams not only in appearance but also demeanor. He is soft-spoken and friendly. I tell him about my breakdown. I'm considering buying a truck to haul the bike home.

He picks up on my depression and tries to cheer me up. "I once broke down in California and hauled my scooter home in the back of a gutted out wagoneer that I bought for $300. I still have that truck and it is my favorite vehicle, next to my Harley."

I am beginning to feel better. I envy the sense of community that I am seeing among this club. I ask, "Just how ugly do you have to be to be an Ugly?"

"You can't just be ugly, you have to really **want** to be Ugly."

Out of the blue, an old man comes up to us and gives us a blueberry pie and drives away. I forget all of my woes as we share the sweet treat.

After the Uglies leave, I help several other people with minor problems, hoping to keep their bikes out of the shop so the mechanics will have more time to work on mine. As closing time approaches I realize that they aren't even going to look at my bike today. I'm furious and give them a piece of my mind. The least they could have done is told me so I could have taken it apart myself and found the problem.

I grab my pack and walk away looking for a room. Most are too expensive. Finally, I discover a hostel with laundry and a bed for ten dollars. Hostels are an interesting alternative to camping and hotels. Dormitory style sleeping with kitchen access for about ten dollars is usual. The clientele is usually international since Europeans are more aware of these facilities. I meet people from France, Germany, Ireland, Australia, and Japan. Most are hitchhiking and each has an exciting story from the road to share. Hitchhiking is more common here and in Canada than in Lower Forty-eight. All the sickos and crazies have scared them all off in the states. I think that trekking across the country on foot would be an excellent way to travel, a real adventure.

The sleeping room is a small basement with the beds crammed next to each other so close that it seems like one long bed on each end of the room. There are two small windows, boarded up and covered with blankets so we can sleep better under the midnight sun. There is no separate room for men and women. This allows a couple who met hitchhiking to sleep together. I walk in on them and they show little embarrassment. In our introductions, I find out that he is from Ireland and she is from Australia. They have matching red hair and accents. She has a bad cold, so I give her some cold pills from my first aid kit.

July 12, Fairbanks, Alaska

I sleep in, enjoying the artificial darkness, and show up at the shop at about 10:00 am, my bike is fixed. The nut on my front sprocket was loose, but no damage was done. A little locktite and she is as good as new. They only charge me $15 for the labor. My lecture last night had an effect.

I change my oil and buy groceries before heading south toward Denali National Park, also known as Mount McKinley—the highest point in North America, 20,320 feet. Along the way I stop near Nenana at Skinny Dick's Halfway Inn. I have a couple of beers and engage in a conversation with Dick and the other locals. Dick looks exactly like you would expect a man named Skinny Dick to look like, his wrinkled face looks almost black in the low light and his Adam's apple hangs from his neck like a lone nugget of gold in a greasy leather poke. He looks like he could die any day. The other men sitting at the bar have equally rugged looks, suggesting lives of hardship and adventure. The topics of conversation reveal little about their personalities. They talk of football, speculating who will be in the Super Bowl this year. The season hasn't even started. They want my insight on the potential of the Dallas Cowboys since I am from Texas. They eye me with suspicion after I admit no interest in the sport. Trying to steer the conversation toward unique "Alaskan" topics to gain insight into the souls of these men, I am met with blank stares and condescending glares. Finally one asks me, "Do you even know what a sourdough is?"

Trying to flatter him, I respond, "Someone who has been in Alaska longer than most, someone who has paid his dues so to speak. Someone like you." I hope my response will initiate stories of the experiences of these men, revealing the essence of life in Alaska.

He responds with a cliché that I have read in every guidebook and brochure on the North Country, "No, stupid! It's someone who's sour on Alaska and too short on dough to get out."

Everyone laughs, not at his joke but at me. These men will not allow themselves to be an attraction so I continue my journey south.

The road to Denali hosts few towns and sparse traffic, I ride hard encouraged by wide shoulders and few frost heaves. The sun is intense and soon I am riding without my jacket, the first time since Montana. The rolling landscape offers a wide panorama interrupted by distant mountain ranges. The Nenana River cuts through the landscape like a hungry bulldozer, leaving a golden curtain of sharp cliffs. Soon the sky begins to cloud up again, the sun pokes through in various places illuminating distant landscapes like a slide show in a dark room. As I get closer to the park, the Alaska Range begins to grow in front of me, guarding the entrance to the park.

It was here, just outside the park boundary, in the summer of 1992, that a young man named Chris McCandless met his fate in the surrounding wilderness. McCandless was an educated idealist who came to the Alaskan bush to escape society and "kill the false being within and victoriously conclude the spiritual pilgrimage." He managed to survive on a few pounds of rice and game he killed with a .22 rifle for over a hundred days. Near the end, after deciding to return to civilization, he was unable to ford the rising waters of the Teklanika River. Returning to his base camp, he accidentally ate the seed pods of a poisonous wild pea. Weak from the poison, unable to hunt, he died of starvation in his sleeping bag 113 days after he entered the bush. His decomposing body was found by hunters 20 days later. The wilderness has taken many others never to be heard of again. There is little room for error when challenging nature.

I heard the McCandless story from Rocky Gilbert, a year before I started this trip. Rocky is an eccentric economics professor at South Dakota State University. I never had any classes with Rocky but his reputation as a free spirit was almost as well known on campus as his tough grading. Passing "Rockenomics" was a feat worth bragging. During Christmas of 1992, I was visiting a friend who was still going to school and I mentioned the possibility of someday going to Alaska on my bike. He told me that Rocky had gone on his Kawasaki that past summer. When I visited his office and told him that I might be considering riding to Alaska he got a crazy passionate look on his face. "Do it! You gotta go! It will change your life!" We spent the next three hours going over maps and photos. By the time I left his office, I was ready to go. I never had a second thought.

In addition to the information on the Alcan, Rocky shared a complete file of clippings about McCandless. It seems that McCandless had spent several months working at a grain elevator near the University, but this proximity was not the only reason the story fascinated Rocky. "We have a lot in common. Non-traditional and looking for ways to live free in spite of the system. That kid had a lotta guts."

I pull into Denali Village late in the evening, feeling completely surrounded by the wilderness. Nearing the park boundary I am confronted with a terrible sight. For about three miles the shoulder of the highway, along the Nenana river, is packed with hundreds of RV's. Campsites are very limited in the area so people just park wherever they please. I pull into the park village pessimistic about my chances of finding a place to sleep. While pondering my situation a couple of drunk women come up. They are seasonal employees from one of the lodges. They show me a side road where I can set up my tent along a small creek. We share a bottle of bourbon and a cold pizza before going back into town for some live music and dancing.

The scene at the lodge is almost as bad as the RVs along the highway, but the bar is definitely not a tourist hangout. It is full of seasonal employees, river rafters, and other assorted park groupies. Most consider themselves some sort of outdoor gurus, trying to prove they are cool. This is their park, all others are intruders. They are philosophizing and complaining about the tourists who supply their bread and butter. I threaten their individuality; compared to me they all look pretty much the same. I am eyed with suspicion, but I'm not staying long—to their relief and mine. While here I am a tourist. I want to see a grizzly and the mountain and then I will be finished with this place.

At midnight, I head back to my tent along the creek. I have finally developed a good system for sleeping. My first concern is hanging my food away from my tent and out of reach of any bears that might wander through camp. I have a rope tied to a bag. After filling the bag with sand, I throw it over a tree and hoist my food at least fifteen feet off the ground. My compact tent is set up on a heavy ground cloth. Inside I roll out my sleeping bag and pad. All of my clothes are put into stuff sacks and rolled inside my jacket, this will serve as my pillow. I sleep next to a can of pepper mace to avert bears and a three foot piece of logging chain to avert anybody else. I have never had to use either. I always wake wondering where in the hell I am and what I'm doing here. Tomorrow, for the first time, I will wake knowing exactly where I am and what I'm doing here, feeling like this tent is my home.

July 13, Denali National Park

I get up early in the morning to reserve a spot on the park's transit system. You can only drive the first fifteen miles of park highway. From that point on access is limited to keep the park wild. Buses with reserved seating take visitors through the park, a good idea in my eyes. At the visitor center I am greeted by a line of about two hundred people, all of them wanting to get into the park. The waiting list is two days for a seat, but a camping spot is available for tomorrow. A camping site guarantees a seat on the bus. I can easily kill a day in the park so I take the site.

After escaping the visitor center, I drive the first fifteen miles of the park road. I see a moose, but the mountain is obscured by clouds. Visitors have only about a 20 percent chance of seeing Denali since most days it is covered by clouds; the huge mass of perpetual snow creates its own weather systems.

The forest here is called Taiga, a Russian word describing the stunted growth of the trees due to the short growing season at these latitudes. The forest is composed of mostly spruce but as the road nears treeline it gradually transforms to stubby willow and alder. These shrubs continue to shrink until they finally become part of the variety of small plants hiding in the carpeted surface of the tundra.

On the way out of the park I stop and see an interesting sled dog demonstration. The park is considered true wilderness so, with the exception of the one road, no motor vehicles are allowed. During the winter sleds are the only practical means of patrolling the park. Each animal has its own dog house, roped off from tourists and the next dog, to prevent fights. Most sit on their houses, indifferent to the whistles and cooing of the people trying to get them to come closer. These dogs are not pets; they are beasts of burden. They do not seem to enjoy being an attraction, much like the men at Skinny Dick's.

After leaving the park, I drive part of the Denali Highway, a 136 mile gravel road that connects Cantwell and Paxton. This road is famous for its excellent views of Denali. Looking to the west I see only clouds but gradually notice that one of them is slightly different. I am looking at the mountain camouflaged by a cloak of clouds. I wait patiently and am rewarded with a clear view of the snowcapped peak. Even from a hundred miles away it dominates the landscape. Staring at this wonder, I try to imagine what it would be like to be one of the people who are, right now, trying to ascend the peak. Basking in the warm sun, the thoughts of camping in subzero weather chill me. Mountaineering is a sport that I do not care to engage in.

I have a can of tuna and crackers for lunch. I think canned tuna is the perfect food. Open the can and eat or you can even cook it. Tuna is really under rated. Order a grilled tuna steak sometime and you'll appreciate the taste more. Best of all it is filling. So filling that I lie down and fall asleep right in the road ditch.

After napping in front of the glowing white mountain, I take a walk on the tundra. Choosing a low lying bowl, I find myself walking on islands of moss and lichens floating on a few inches of water; tussocks or hummocks, I don't think there is any difference. Standing still, my feet sink several inches into this elegant, pulpy carpet. It is quite difficult to move on this mushy, unstable surface. This "wet" tundra is quite fragile, any disturbance from people walking or moose feeding causes some of the plants to die. If enough plants are killed, these darker dead plants will absorb enough heat to allow a thawing of the frozen soil below. The meadow is dotted with small, deep potholes, most no larger than a basketball, created by disturbances. Hopping over these miniature lakes, I notice that each holds a small community of insects which I study until my bent back begins to ache. I wonder if I could come back here in a few years and see a trail of lakes created by my footsteps.

Walking on the tundra, I discovered that the soles of my boots are wore out. Cold water seeped through and soaked the bottoms of my feet. I have a bad habit of dragging my feet on the highway when taking off. I expected these boots to go and have packed an extra pair. Planning on throwing these away, I decide to drop my feet onto the pavement flying under my bike, something I have always wanted to do. The road is always right there but blurred by the speed, my eyes can't focus on it. Sometimes it seems fluid as it flies past. Cautiously, I touch the road at 45 miles per hour, afraid of twisting an ankle. A buzz and a tickling vibration on the bottoms of my feet announce my contact with the highway. I speed up to 55, then 65, the same sensation. The road is definitely there and it is solid. At 70 the friction heats up my soles and the rubber begins to melt. Suddenly, I realize that this is stupid. I could break my ankles doing this and I'm not paying attention to my driving. Sometimes the child in each of us takes over and we do things for no apparent reason. One time riding through a canyon in Colorado, I spotted a rock in the road. Without thinking, I extended my foot to kick it off. Speeding down the highway most things are larger than they appear. This rock was; my stubbed toe turned blue and hurt for a month.

Before setting up camp for the night, I decide to stop by a store for groceries. The woman working the till compliments my bike. Seil's eyes sparkle in her flawless tanned face as we talk. She is beautiful, a perpetual smile consumes her whole face. Her curly auburn hair is slightly windblown, but not messy. As the conversation progresses I find out that she rode all the way up here alone, from South Carolina, on a Honda Shadow, in May! Hard core, she must have froze her bottom off. I dream of marrying a woman like her someday.

July 14, Denali Village

Since I'm only going into the park for one night, I pack light, leaving all my extra gear with the owners of the campground where I stayed last night. My throat is getting sore, so I stop at a store to get some hard candy to suck on. The girl from the hostel in Fairbanks gave me her cold.

I leave my bike at Riley Creek Campground and catch my bus. The driver's name is Dick. Sitting behind the huge steering wheel the smallness of his features is exaggerated. Most of his serious face is hidden by a gray beard and hair. He has a harsh dry humor that I appreciate. "This is a camper bus not a tourist bus. We are not going to stop for every caribou or sheep that we see sitting on a hill five miles away. We will stop for quality not quantity. I will not tell you the names of every stupid feature of the park since you probably don't care. If you have a question ask, otherwise I'll shut up so you can enjoy the park on your terms not mine."

At one of the checkpoints waits a couple of backpackers who, judging by their inadequate equipment, have no business in the backcountry. I recognize them from the waiting line at the visitor center. I overheard the man say, "We aren't going to wait two days to get on a bus, we're buying a backcountry permit and going in today. How hard can it be."

The father and his daughter are totally soaked from a river crossing. I guess they found out how hard it can be. Each bus starts the day with a few open seats to allow people who are already in the park to travel from place to place. Dick looks at them and says, "You can get on the next bus, I don't want you or your smelly gear on my bus." Right on Dick!

I get off at Sanctuary Campground and set up my tent quickly, hoping to catch the next bus. I have to wait only about ten minutes, but it turns out to be a tourist bus. The driver names every rock and creek till I am sick of her voice; we stop for every rock that the lady across from me swears is a bear. The bus, leased from the Fairbanks school district, has high backed seats for safety, but they block all the views, forcing all the passengers to constantly crane their necks and jump up at any indication of something exciting. There is a constant tension in the air, a competition to see who will get the best views. Any window seat is guarded carefully by the owner. Most of the passengers are anxious, knowing that this might be their only chance to see a bear—ever. Scanning the tundra, their eyes show a nervous urgency, like a mother searching for a lost child in a shopping mall.

Stopping at Eilson Visitor Center, I notice the incredible variety of mountains here. A few conservative rolling hills and some flat topped plateaus. One ridge looks like the ruffled feathers of a chicken that has been rubbed the wrong way. Another looks like the dissolving foam on the edge of a dirty lake. Snow lies on many of the peaks like toilet paper hanging in trees after Halloween, the remnants of childish pranks. Sunset Peak, with glaciers flowing off the top, rises above a flat green valley with a river winding through like a thousand silver ribbons blowing in the wind. Denali looms directly above, demanding my attention. Clouds filter the views of the peak, allowing only picture puzzle sections. Looking up through them reveals a glacier here and a sharp peak there. A little lower a rugged ridge shows its face. It is like seeing the mountain through a movie camera, panning over one section at a time, but never revealing the whole story. I sit and watch the perpetually changing view while eating my lunch.

The verdant valley below Sunset Peak seems larger than the sky itself, projecting the shadow from each cloud above. The valley calls me. I cross the road and head down a ridge leading toward the peak. Since there are no trails in the park, I have to bust my way through some of the thickest brush I have ever seen. Sometimes my feet are not even touching the ground, I just hop from willow to willow to alder. The whole time banging rocks together and yelling, "Hey bear, Hey bear!" I don't want to surprise any grizzlies. Park rangers say that the bears are unpredictable, sows with cubs being the most dangerous. If a bear charges do not run. To the simple minded beasts running means prey, eat. Stand your ground and talk in a calm voice, telling the bear you are not food, as if he understands. Wait till the last minute and (as you piss your pants) fall down on your belly and put your hands behind your head to protect your spine. In the end if the bear wants to eat you it will. Here nature rules on its terms not ours.

In a way I want to see a grizzly on this hike, it is the only way to really understand the true nature of this wilderness. The moment that you realize that the bear is in control you begin to understand. The only time I have come close to this experience was hiking in South Dakota and unknowingly walking up to a buffalo. I no longer had a say in my fate; it was all up the that old bull. Instead of charging, he turned and walked away, leaving me alone with my pounding heart.

The rangers discourage hiking alone, but I prefer experiencing nature this way. The wilderness is shy and groups of people intimidate it. Alone you can mingle and converse with the wild. I want to listen to what the tundra has to say, not some idiot I just met. I wade across a stream and work my way up the steep bank to the plateau above. I spend more than an hour laying on my belly like a child exploring the tundra plants and frozen soil of the permafrost below. This is "dry" tundra, no water here. The layer of plants on the top of the frozen soil is thin. Low bush cranberries, dogwoods, and other woody plants share space with sedges, lichens, and mosses. Finding a flat rock, I chop a hole into the solid ground. Holding my hand in this frozen cave, I try to feel the antiquity of this soil that has never thawed.

I walk back to the visitor center, sucking on a rock to relieve my burning throat. I catch the first bus back to Sanctuary. On the way home my cold gets worse, but we start to see wildlife in abundance: moose, caribou, and Dall sheep. After a while, I quit announcing the animals that I spot, wanting to get back to camp and get some rest. One caribou has its nose stuck in a snowbank, trying to keep insects from entering its nostrils and laying eggs. Several species of insects plague the caribou, biting them and laying their eggs in any orifice they can find. Often entire herds of them can be seem running wildly trying to escape the assaults from their tiny aggressors.

While watching the miserable caribou I notice four light brown spots moving on the mountainside in the distance. The driver confirms the grizzlies. It is a sow with three yearling cubs. Each as big as her, it is hard to call them cubs. Watching them, I realize how quickly and easily they move through the bush that posed such a barrier to my hike. They cover two miles in about fifteen minutes.

They disappear in a draw, but the bus driver sits patiently. Shortly, they emerge just a hundred yards from us. I am ecstatic—seeing these animals in the wild—yet the view from the safety of the bus dilutes the experience. It seems little different than a zoo except we are in the cage looking out at the bear instead of the opposite. I can now leave the park having seen what I came to see—a grizzly and the mountain.

July 15, Sanctuary Campground

Two hours before the first bus is scheduled to arrive, I wake with my throat on fire. A short hike kills time before the my ride arrives. As we near the park boundary, I feel like I have just finished a ride at an amusement park. Back to the real world. I am overjoyed when I see my bike. After being on it for twenty-four days this stretch of a little more than twenty-four hours off of it has given me separation anxiety. I walk around it, carefully checking to be sure nobody has messed with my baby.

I ride to the commercial campground and I pick up the gear I left, carefully packing it on my bike. Heading south toward Anchorage, the highway offers some excellent views of Denali and the Alaska Range but today most of the views are obscured by low dark clouds threatening to rain.

As I near the city, the buildings get trashier and trashier. It starts looking like the Southern U.S. where people never throw anything away and never take the time to check the spelling on the signs they paint. In Trinity we have "Linda's Dinner" instead of "Diner" (only open for breakfast and lunch) and more backward "Ss" and "Ns"than you can attribute to simple stencil errors. Then I see the sign, "Houston, Alaska;" I can't resist the photo opportunity.

Just outside the Anchorage city limits a bunch of Harleys are parked at a campground. I pull in and am welcomed by the Fairbanks Harley Owner's Group (HOG) chapter. I recognize many of them from my time at the dealer in Fairbanks. Unlike most HOG chapters, expensive new Evolutions are not the most common bikes here. They drive a variety of older, personalized bikes, mostly pre-1980 shovelheads and a few old iron-head Sportsters. Sitting around the camp, they tell of hard core Alaskan winter rides, producing pictures to prove it. I get cold just looking at the photos of riders in twenty below, snowy weather. They are a very down to earth group, much different than the country club atmosphere of many HOG chapters. They are here for the First Alaskan State HOG Rally. I decide to camp with them and take in the rally.

Going to a rally requires a change in attitude from my solo road riding. I prepare to meet all kinds of bikers and socalize as another face in the crowd rather than one that stands out. Within the biking sub-culture there are several types of riders. First are the hard core old-timers who were riding before Harleys were popular, like most of the folks in this Fairbanks group. They are usually laid back and humbly refer to their bikes as scooters. In contrast to them are the new RUBs (Rich Urban Bikers.) They have money to burn, a Harley is a toy to flaunt their wealth and pick up women. Somewhere in between are those, like myself, who own their bikes to ride them. We don't feel right unless we are going somewhere. On the far end of the spectrum are the outlaws or "One Percenters." The American Motorcycle Association says that ninety-nine percent of bikers are good people and only one percent are "rotten apples." The outlaws proudly wear patches that proclaim "1%er." They force their rules of conduct upon all other bikers and you would be a fool to stand in their way.

HOG rallies try to cater to all groups, excluding the One Percenters, but tend to favor the new wave of RUBs who bring lots of money and are willing to spend it. This will be a bit of a change for me but after so many days on the road I am ready to slow down and socialize a little. It will also give me a needed break to try to shake my cold.

Trying to register at the rally, I am given a run around by rally officials who doubt my membership since I don't carry a HOG card. Finally convincing them of my honesty, I pay my $20 registration fee. The rally is lame, but I meet a few interesting people. First are Clint and Lynne Seyer who designed the rally T-shirt that I couldn't get because I didn't preregister. Clint draws his design in my journal, a cartoon bear on a bike.

Soon, I hear my name over the loud speakers. I am being called on stage. They give me a consolation prize since Texas is the second biggest state and I am now in the biggest state. I am presented with a giant foam novelty cowboy hat. I don't bother to tell them that I am not a native Texan and eventually throw away the hat.

Ditching the rally and heading out on a ride around the city, I am disappointed to discover that there is little unique about Anchorage. If you blindfolded someone and flew them here, I doubt that they would know they were in Alaska. The attitudes of the people here are much different than those of the rest of the state. They seem just like any other urbanites I have met from Houston or Los Angeles or wherever. The city has malls, factories, freeways, and traffic; all things I want to escape. The Chugach Range and, in the distance, Denali remind the residents that they are in Alaska, depressing the many who will never leave the city and tempting many others to leave and never come back.

I retreat to the Log Cabin Tavern, not far from my campground. Most of the waitresses here ride. In fact, Alaska has more motorcycles, more Harleys, and more woman riders, per capita, than any other state. Quite impressive considering they only have a three month riding season.

I spend the bulk of the evening standing around a campfire, enjoying the conversation of the guys from Fairbanks. When I first come into contact with any new group of bikers I am cautious. I sit back and listen and observe until I can decide for sure what type of group I am dealing with. Making the wrong comment to the wrong group will make you look like a moron or get you ostracized from the group. If you are dealing with One Percenters you could get stomped simply for wearing the wrong kind of patch on your jacket.

I got my Harley, brand new, at Sturgis, the largest motorcycle rally in the world. I thought I was so cool riding down the strip on my bare bones Sportster with giant dealer plates. I pulled into the Broken Spoke Saloon, where you can ride you bike into the bar, and ordered a beer to celebrate my graduation into the world of "Cool." After finishing my brew I got back on my bike and warmed it up. Suddenly it died. I started it up again and began to pull out. It died again and would not start back up. I cranked and cranked, wearing down the battery, cussing the whole time. Finally this greasy old guy next to me shouts, "Turn on the gas, asshole!" It takes more than a bike and a leather jacket to make you cool. I had a lot to learn.

Sitting around the campfire, I causally make a comment about some situation "back in the States." I am sharply reminded by the Fairbanks group that I still am in the U.S. I am afraid I have made a major mistake but quickly realize that this is a common slip made by outsiders. It is an Alaska thing not a biker thing and I have retained my "Cool." This spurs a whole conversation on Alaska's alienation by the Lower Forty-eight.

"I hate it when I order something and they charge me foreign shipping, I try to tell them that Alaska is in the U.S. but they have their policies and they never concede." Alaskans will use the phrase "in the States" causally but if you are not from Alaska, a little more caution is expected. I quickly learn to use "Lower Forty-eight."

July 16, Anchorage

I head back to the rally. I don't know what my $20 entry fee was for, since they charge five dollars for the door prize drawings and fifteen dollars for the dance tonight. Just for fun I enter my bike in the show with all my muddy gear tied on it. Several people come up to me saying, "I voted for your bike because it is a real bike, not a polished show bike."

One HOG member arrives on a BMW. His Harley is broke down; they won't let him into the rally on anything but a Harley. During the field events a crowd of onlookers assembles. Rather than letting these people in and showing them some biker hospitality, the rally officials make them watch from behind a chain link fence. I can't tell if they are caged out or I'm caged in.

Most of the people here are great but the rally is boring. I hook up with Franklin from Barrow, the northernmost town in Alaska, and Eric from Maryland. Franklin works for an oil company, two weeks on and one off. He comes to Anchorage where he has an apartment and his Harley. Spending his time off riding and partying during the summer and traveling the world during the winter, he escapes the bleak environment of the North Slope. Eric beats me out for distance rider, his bleached hair and sunburned face testify to the length of time he has been on the road. We soon find out that we are good riding partners and enjoy practicing useless riding skills like waiting at stoplights without putting our feet down, simply balancing on two wheels.

We spend the night bar hopping and finally end up at a cabaret. Several bikes parked out front beacon us. We are inside before we realize it is a strip bar, but we decide to stay for a beer before calling it a night. Actually I have a soda, my cold is still dragging me down. Before long we meet Taren, a slim blond dancer who looks like she could still be in high school. She joins our table for the evening, offering table dances, but we decline. Before we know it, she is doing one anyway, no charge. The strip joint turns into a way for us to defy the rally by doing our own thing, something immoral. It is a way for us to assert our anonymity. The dancers have made up names and fake affection, and we treat them like they are the most wonderful, beautiful women we have ever seen. It is all an act. It is sad but true, these kind of bars always attract a lot of bikers.

July 17, Anchorage

Before leaving Anchorage, I meet Bert. Originally from Austria, he came here three years ago and has not been able to leave; he loves it here. His simple clean "no frills" bike won the Rider's Choice award at the rally, testimony to the sensibilities of the local bikers who were not impressed with other bikes that, although fancier, are not really ridden by their owners. Working as a driver for the local beer distributor, Bert is the perfect guide to local bars. After hitting a few in town, we head south down the Kenai Peninsula for beers at the Bird House Bar.

The Bird House is about 25 miles south of Anchorage on the Seward Highway. The 1964 Good Friday earthquake caused considerable damage in the area. The surrounding land sunk into the sea, turning forests into salt water marshes with skeleton trees poking out. The Bird House sunk too and remains half buried in the hillside. No description can prepare you for the interior of this local landmark. It is the trashiest place I have ever been in. I loved it!

For years patrons have stapled business cards, bras, panties, jock straps, and just about anything else you can imagine on the walls. Layers upon layers have accumulated to the point that the walls feel as spongy as the surrounding tundra. The dirt and sawdust floor is so uneven that I feel drunk before finishing my first beer. The severe angle of the bar causes any unattended drink to slide away from the careless owner. Locals bring rubber mats to hold their drinks.

Nothing at the Bird House is as it seems, the place is loaded with practical jokes. I fall for a bathroom door with a fake knob on the hinged side. I'm waiting for it to be unlocked when a local cuts in front of me and pushes on the "wrong" side of the door, it opens. I use the utmost caution the rest of the afternoon letting others be the butt of the jokes.

Alone again and heading south, I round the tip of Turnagin Arm, one of the most dangerous bodies of water in the world. All along the way signs exclaim "Dangerous Quicksand." I inquire about the signs at a nearby roadhouse.

When the tide is out the mud flats along the arm look inviting but much of the "sand" is actually glacial silt. This fine silt, when mixed with water becomes dangerous quicksand. This, combined with the fact that the tides can sweep over the mud flats as fast as 15 miles per hour, creates a potentially fatal situation. I heard unconfirmed rumors of a woman stuck in the mud, submerged by the tide, breathing through a snorkel, and finally dying of hypothermia. Another rumor tells of a soldier stuck in the mud, being pulled in half by a helicopter trying to save him from the advancing tide. I stay off the flats.

The road rises above the bay as I feel my bladder filling up. Stopping along a side road to relieve myself, I hear repeated gunshots back on the highway. Local kids shooting signs. All over the state I have noticed holes blasted in all the signs. More than I have ever seen anywhere else. It seems to me that in a state with so many hunting opportunities that people would not have to shoot signs. It also seems that in a state where most people are against taxation, they would have a little more respect for public property. Maybe they are rebelling against anything "public" or maybe they are just bored.

I head west on the Sterling Highway toward Cooper Landing where my friend Stacy, from Texas, is working for the U.S. Fish and Wildlife Service this summer. Signs for the Kenai National Wildlife Refuge tell me I am getting close. I pull into her yard and am welcomed by a familiar face. She introduces me to her roommates, they welcome me from a cautious distance. She explains, "You look pretty scary, Al." In the bathroom I look myself over in the mirror. Pieces of skin are peeling off my sunburnt nose. My untrimmed beard has blown out in all directions. Trying to pull it back into my face, chunks of caked mud fall into the sink. Greasy hair lies flat on my skull. After soaking my aching muscles in the bath, I have to rinse in the shower before I feel clean. I rake my hair and find some Q-tips, the cotton comes out of my ear black. Several swabs are required to dig all of the soil out of my ears. Half of Canada came here with me! Stacy's roommates warm up to me after my wash. I am treated with a baked salmon dinner while sharing my adventures. Stacy brings me up to date on events in Texas. She talks with a twinkle in her eye and music in her voice. I am comforted by her familar face and it is obvious that she is happy to see me.

July 18, Cooper Landing

Stacy is working on a backcountry trail crew this summer. They pack into the refuge wilderness and repair any damage they find on the trails along the way. I am hoping to sign on as a volunteer and go with them for a few days but soon find out that this plan has fallen through. I spend the day sitting around the trailer, doing laundry, but mostly resting. After so many days without the media, the evil television hypnotizes me, wasting my day.

After a halibut dinner we go to Gwin's Lodge for beers. Alaskan Amber, brewed in Juneau, is the drink of choice. It is a very tasty brew, but for $11 a pitcher it better be. I almost haven't noticed the gradual increases in prices as I have traveled north. Beers are regularly $4 each and a cup of soup can be the same price. I have bought breakfasts for $7 thinking they were a bargain. In Anchorage gas is a reasonable $1.20 a gallon, fifteen miles out of town it is $1.40, fifty miles out of town it is $1.60. When you have no choice you have to pay for it.

The diverse backgrounds of the Fish and Wildlife employees makes for a lot of interesting conversation. We quickly cover the obvious topics: moose, salmon, bears, and, of course, the long days. Since it has not been getting dark and I have not been carrying a watch, I was unaware of the changes in my sleeping habits. Midnight feels like 10:00 p.m. We go to bed at 2:00 am yet I am up again by 7:00 am. Even locals have been known to suffer from this phenomena, staying awake for several days and then collapsing from lack of sleep.

Soon the conversation turns to more important topics such as what really is the best beer in the world. We never reach a consensus but all agree that the topic requires more research. Jim, is the oldest in the crowd and reminds me of one of my uncles. We find a common interest in Native American lore and history. It is relaxing to be around friends and reassures me of the sanity of my trip. I have found a destination.

July 19, Cooper Landing

With all the gear off of my bike, I enjoy traveling the backroads of the area. It feels like a completely different machine, light and responsive. On the main highway I take it up to 85 mph, enjoying the unrestrained power. I stop at Skilack Lake and hike to a ridge overlooking the lake and the surrounding valley. Hoping to spot a bear, I sit on this high vantage point with binoculars watching the wildlife activity for several hours. I am eager to spot something here—outside park boundaries—where seeing bears is not a daily occurrence.

A small rocky island on the lake below shelters a bird rookery. The gulls and other birds produce an incredible din, whitewashing the rocks with defecation. On the north end, the lake empties into a wide channel of intertwined streams. I find it easy to imagine the glacier that carved out this wide valley. In these streams and the surrounding marshes and lakes are several moose feeding as they wallow through the muck. Giving up on the bears, I turn my attention to the surrounding mountainsides, hoping to spot some sheep.

After a couple of hours, I head back down the trail. On the way, I watch little gray birds hop from tree to tree and later follow a family of grouse through the brush. "Devil's club" is a dominate plant here in the wet climate. It is a mean looking, thorny plant with huge leaves. It looks worse than it actually is. In Texas we have a plant called "Devil's walking stick," it is much worse. It has sharp woody spikes all the way up its trunk. This small tree will reach out and grab you and tear your clothes and skin to shreds. Luckily, it is not as prevalent as the Devil's club is here.

Before heading back to Stacy's, I stop by one of the many small lakes that dot the landscape. I am rewarded with the haunting evening songs of loons. Their long mournful cries send a shiver up my spine as I watch them glide across the glassy cobalt waters.

July 20, Cooper Landing

Stacy has the day off so we plan a sightseeing cruise out of Seward. A co-worker, Rob, and his friend, Mark, join us. Luckily we pick one of the best cruises in Alaska, Kenai Fjords.

The charter boat takes us throughout Kenai Fjords National Park. We leave Seward early in the morning under questionable weather. Soon after departing, we are greeted by sea otters floating near kelp beds. These cute mammals dive deep below the surface of the icy water protected by the densest fur in the animal kingdom. On the bottom they find a variety of clams that they break open on their bellies with rocks.

Not long after leaving the otters, the captain points out a humpback whale in the distance. Humpbacks are baleen whales, filtering plankton or krill out of the water with brushlike plates that hang inside their mouths. Sometimes they catch schools of small fish in a bubble net. The whales swim below the school blowing bubbles that rise to the surface. The bubbles surround and confuse the fish. The whales swim up the center of the trap, gulping down the entire school. It takes over two tons of food a day to nourish their huge 60 foot long bodies. We watch anxiously, hoping to see the whale breach completely out of the water. Some researchers think this act is employed to knock barnacles off the whale's skin. Others think it is just for fun. Before moving on we see the whale break the surface of the water several times, but it never completely breaches. The captain assures us that we will see more whales as we head out into open waters.

As we leave the protected waters of Resurrection Bay the winds pick up and the large ship is tossed back and forth. I see the first of many people puking off the back. Before returning to quieter waters, I will begin to feel a bit queezy myself. We are finally rewarded for our discomfort by the sight of fin whales, the second largest whale, next to blues. Fin whales communicate with other whales throughout the ocean, sending out signals that can be heard up to 2,000 miles away.

After observing the whales, we head to the Chiswell Islands—site of an incredible puffin rookery. At least four different species of birds nest here, each occupying a different niche on the cliffs of these islands. The island we approach is called Beehive not only because of its steep sides and rounded top, but also for the incredible number of birds swarming around the cliffs. The captain brings the ship within about twenty yards of the rocky walls. We identify horned and tuffted puffins, mures, kittywinks, and auklets. All are very short, stout birds with wings so short that flying would seem impossible. The swarming birds shit in the faces of many of the people looking up at them, protesting our presence so close to their coveted nests.

Many of the islands with more conservative slopes host colonies of seals and sea lions. The noise from these numbers of animals can be deafening. Unlike the otters, they protect themselves from the cold through a thick layer of blubber.

We move on to our final stop, Holgate Glacier. Miles before reaching the face of this mass of ice, we feel the temperature begin to drop until the air is near freezing. Soon small chunks of blue ice begin to appear, floating on the dark water like blue jewels lying on black velvet. Rounding the final bend, we see another charter boat dwarfed by the immense river of ice. The ice dissapears into the low clouds, making the glacier seem to rise all the way to the heavens.

I do not realize the dynamics of the glacier until the captain kills the engines. The sounds are incredible; continual creaks, groans, and pops can be heard over the background of rushing water. Suddenly, there is a sharp crack followed by the rumble of falling ice. The calving climaxes with an explosion of ice against water. I am in awe the entire time we float in front of this spectacle.

The crew scoops up a load of small icebergs and dumps them on the deck, allowing us to study and feel the product of snows from centuries before. I suck on a small piece. It tastes like a regular ice cube. The only difference is the clarity, it is perfectly transparent. It is this transparency that gives the larger chunks their deep blue color. The absence of color makes them beautiful. It is like looking at the edge of a thick pane of glass, no matter how clear is looks from the front, the edge is always deep blue-green.

On the return trip, we are again greeted by the humpback whale who allows us a much closer look before she flips her tail and waves good-bye. We return home, exhausted from the magnitude of these experiences.

July 21, Cooper Landing

Waking early in the morning, Stacy, Mark, Rob, and I head to the beaches south for the low tide, perfect clamming. I have never clammed but it sounds fun. We arrive at the appropriately named Clam Gulch right at low tide, ready to get our limit of "razors."

We walk the beach with shovel and bucket looking for a small dimple in the sand. The challenge has been made, I quickly start a hole with the shovel and then continue with my bare hands. The clam magically slides deep into the sand. If I am quick enough I get a hold of its "foot." It stretches as I pull, but eventually lets go and joins my harvest in the bucket.   I become so engrossed in the hunt that I do not realize that the tide is coming in. When I finally look up, my point of land is no longer a point, I am surrounded by water. I quickly make my retreat with the cold water only a hair away from the top of my waders.

Since I have purchased a 24-hour fishing license for clamming, I decide to get in a little salmon fishing while I'm legal. Rob's friend, Mark is my guide. Mark is only a little more familiar with the area than I, but he knows how to fish, I don't. Fishing for salmon is not really fishing, it's actually snagging. You stand along the stream, floating your "lure" down the bottom with the current, hoping to catch a salmon with its mouth open. If you snag it anywhere but its mouth it's not legal and you throw it back. I don't have to worry, I don't snag any.

The evening is not wasted, the waters of the Kenai River are as beautiful as any; glacial silt makes the water emerald green, opaque not transparent. The rocky bottom of this river creates dangerous looking whitewater and eddies. Directly in front of me sits a large standing wave, it is constantly moving, changing, yet it remains, rolling over and over in the same spot. While I cast, a bald eagle flies overhead looking for a meal. On the way home we interrupt several moose feeding along the roadside.

July 22, Cooper Landing

Hiking from Stacy's trailer, I take the Resurrection Trail five miles to Juneau Falls. It is a good hike—not too steep, but enough of a rise to be interesting. I climb out on a ledge to get some photos of the falls with fireweed and a variety of other wildflowers in the foreground. The small stream pours clear black water out into a dark gully, producing an impressive fall and a cloud of cool mist. The platy rock that has been exposed by the rushing waters is slippery charcoal gray, shining with a continual coat of water from the falls. The ledges and more moderate slopes have clothed themselves with a rich velvety carpet of mosses, lichens, and other small plants. I am reminded of the sheen of a rich man's smoking jacket, with deep red, brown, and royal green paisley, decorated with wildflowers, like red, violet, and purple jewels. The exposed wet rock becomes the black satin collar, lapels, and cuffs. The mist rises in the air like the smoke from an expensive cigar, strong and rugged yet somehow classy. I am sitting in a dimly lit study, discussing politics with the rocks, trying to understand their elegant perspective. The mountains rising from the mellow green valley above the falls are as distant as a painting on the wall.

From this ledge above, I notice a small aluminum boat folded around a rock on the edge of the falls. It destroys my mood and snaps me back into reality. This is not a navigable stream and it is five miles from the nearest road, what madman brought a boat up here? I climb around until I'm directly above the falls and try to push it over but the rushing water has a tight grip on it. I give up, not willing to risk my life to save a view. Hiking back down the trail, I notice the sky getting dim; I spent a lot more time here than I realized, hypnotized by the motion of the falling water. This whole day the air has held the smell of a fresh dewy morning. I inhale deep breaths trying to capture this aroma in my memory.

July 23, Cooper Landing

I decide to give Stacy and her roommates a break. Without saying anything they have given me indications that they need some space. It has been said that if you really want to enjoy Alaska you must find a friend to stay with and show you around. It has also been said that if you stay for more than a week you won't be invited back. I think this applies to any situation, not just Alaska. I leave some of my gear and head south for a weekend trip to Homer. Homer is the home town of writer and Motel Six spokesperson, Tom Bodett who says, "If you got into your car," (or motorcycle) "in New York and you wanted to take a nice long drive, I mean the *longest* drive you could take without turning around or running into a foreign language, this is where you'd wind up."

The Sterling Highway follows the Cook Inlet through several small towns before it ends in Homer. The salty, wet breeze off the ocean chills and depresses me. I am starting the think I will never see the area under blue skies. When I round the last bend and come into view of the town and Kachemak Bay my spirits are lifted. Mellow peaks rise above wide valleys filled with lazy glaciers. From my elevated position, I can see the narrow Homer spit sliding five miles out into the bay, pointing to the incredible scenery.

Homer is more like two towns. I pass through the "real" town first. It seems pretty much like any other small town, a couple grocery and drug stores, a few bars, and your standard service enterprises. The road goes through town and out onto the spit. The slim strip of land holds mostly restaurants and souvenir stands. A few fishing charters, a cannery, and a hotel fill in the spaces. The rocky beaches are covered with a collage of ratty tents and makeshift shelters, the homes of seasonal cannery workers. Mostly college kids lured here by rumors of $10,000 summers. Nobody gets rich off the canneries, but it's not a bad place to spend a summer.

Following the good advice Bert gave me before we left the Bird House, I pull in to check out the Salty Dawg Saloon. The Salty Dawg is a remodeled lighthouse complete with portholes on walls covered completely with cedar shakes. It barely rises above the surrounding buildings but it definitely stands out. If Bert had not told me about it, I'm sure I would have been drawn to it anyway. Small rooms and low ceilings make the place crowded but homey. I am greeted by two voluptuous women from Salt Lake City who adore bikers. I don't mind being adored. Meanwhile, they are being adored by a local crabber who brings a garbage bag of freshly boiled dungeness crabs. They invite me in on their feast. Soon the women are gone and I am left with a full belly and the crabber, a bag of empty shells.

About to leave and find a campsite, I notice three girls sitting at a table. Dressed in tattered, dirty jeans and tie-dye T-shirts, one even has dread-locks, they don't look like tourists so I strike up a conversation. Peggy, Mary, and Genie (with the dreads), are recent college graduates from Massachusetts. On a road trip before they each begin their quest for a career, they are eager to swap stories from the road.

We enjoy a few games of pool before they offer to cook me dinner. I'm not really hungry but want to spend more time with them before they leave. After telling them of my hopes of finding a way across the bay to hike the wilderness of Kachemak State Park, they reveal similar plans. They have found a crabber who says he will take them across the bay to the trailhead and pick them up in a couple days. I am invited. The trip offers us mountains and glaciers surrounded by rainforests. The maps shows many high-country lakes. Excited about the trip, we stay up all night around a campfire on the beach, enjoying the marathon sunset. It lasts all night, I can not tell when it becomes the sunrise, each day flows into the next. I think too many people live their lives sleeping in, watching the sun set, but never enjoying the sunrise. Always looking to the end and never appreciating the beginning. Here there is no beginning or end, the days casually blend together.

July 24, Homer

I take an early walk along the beach at low tide. Eagles are picking at the carcasses of fish that have been left by the receding water. A girl is wading in a tidal pool near her mother. I find a hermit crab and show it to her. She is afraid at first, not of the crab, but me. She looks toward her mother for approval. Cautiously her mother's eyes say, "It's all right."

Watching the creatures in a tidal pool is like looking at another planet. An incredible variety of creatures sit here waiting for the tides to come and protect them from our intrusions. Here, in these cold waters, I had not expected to find much. There is a colorful variety of hardy creatures that manage to survive in this chilly environment. Many were threatened by oil that was swept into the bay after the Exxon Valdez accident. This beach was hit hard. There is no longer any visible oil but the locals say that just a couple feet below the surface the sand is still saturated. Out of sight but **not** out of mind.

We pack our tents and go to the Salty Dawg to meet our ride across the bay. The crabber never shows. He either wasn't serious or was too drunk to remember. With our plans of a backpacking trip blown, I say good-bye to the girls and head to the Pratt Museum to take my mind off the trip that won't happen. They have interesting displays on aquatic life, the Valdez oil spill, and local plants. A good museum is set apart from the average by interactive displays. The Pratt has them, you don't passively read who donated what; you listen, feel, and respond to their displays.

Through the grapevine on the beach, I hear that the East End Bar has free hors d'oeuvres on Sunday nights, mostly for the locals since the Anchorage tourists have gone home for the week. I see that it is time and head up the road. I gorge myself on barbecue pork chops and a variety of side dishes. Afterward I drive the east highway, the views of this glorious place persisting through a soft haze. The sturdy mountains struggle, holding the dark clouds above, sheltering the precious glaciers cradled below.

On my return trip, I see a cannery worker who is camped next to me hitching a ride. I pick him up to give him a ride back to camp. Not a quarter of a mile after he gets on we pass a gorgeous brunette in a leather jacket with her thumb out. I don't have the heart to dump him off. "Sorry, man," is all he can say.

That night we have a party on the beach complete with Lucky Lager, the only cheap beer in Alaska. Cheap because the bottles are eleven ounces instead of twelve, each case shorts us the equivalent of two bottles. We don't notice the missing ounces. Lucky has picture puzzles inside their caps, so we spend the night trying to find the answers to simple riddles. These kids living here and working the canneries are tough and making the best of life. I admire them.

July 25, Homer

Leaving Homer under a curtain of rain, I head back to Cooper Landing to pick up my gear and bid farewell to Stacy. I have not felt totally comfortable with last couple of days we spent together. I can't put my finger on it, but seeing a friend in a different setting with new friends can be a little unsettling. I graduated from college a couple years before a girl friend of mine. We decided to go our separate ways. I went back to visit her just before she graduated. We had dinner, but could find nothing to talk about. I was uninterested in school and her new friends and she could not relate to my job. The only thing that we ever had in common was the fact that we were going to the same school at the same time. We finally steered the conversation to things from our past and made it through the evening. I have not talked to her since.

Stacy and I go for a midnight walk along the Kenai River, talking of simple things and the beauty of this place. The salmon surfacing in the rushing rapids are at the half way point of their final journey, traveling to spawn where they were born and die. I will start my journey home tomorrow.

July 26, Cooper Landing

I have grown accustomed to the constant drizzle here, but had hoped to see the area under blue skies. As I pull away from Stacy's it starts to rain.

Planning a side trip to Seward to take a hike up to the Harding Icefields, I ride through the rain to the road leading to Exit Glacier. The dirt road is riddled with jarring washboards and coats me and my bike with chalky mud. Labeled as Alaska's most accessible glacier, Exit lies in Kenai Fjords National Park. My hopes of taking the strenuous trail up to the Harding Icefields are shattered when I am confronted by "Trail Closed" signs. At least I will get on the glacier itself.

On the trail to the glacier, interpretive signs suggest, "Look for iceworms on the glacier ice late in the evening." Contrary to popular belief iceworms do exist. The black threadlike creatures live in the ice, feeding on pollen that collects on the surface. The heat from a human touch can cook their delicate bodies.

A cold welcome waits for me at the face of the glacier. The whole area has been roped off, "Dangerous Falling Ice." I came to touch a glacier. Looking for an area that appears safe, I find a hidden trail worn from occasional footsteps along the far side of the glacier. I follow it to the ice but the feeling of discovery has been destroyed by park formalities.

Returning to the viewing area, I am met by a park ranger, "Do you realize that by walking around the barriers, other people will get the idea that it is safe? If a child follows you, you will be responsible." Does he think that by riding a motorcycle, I am also giving people the idea that bikes are safe? Am I responsible for them? Why can't some people accept the fact that others want to live dangerously?

On my way out I reread the sign that suggested going on the ice to look for worms. It is still there so I go to the park office to ask somebody to take me someplace where I *can* see worms. "We don't allow people on the ice, we need to change that sign."

"Why?"

"We had a liability."

"A liability?" I'm curious.

"A woman was looking for worms when a piece of ice fell on her and killed her."

I don't call that a liability, I call that very bad luck.

Fed up with the park scene, I head for the nearest bar, The Yukon. I am welcomed with a wide selection of beers, a free block of cheese, and a cute bartender, Mary. She is busy picking quarters off the floor and from around the bottles of booze behind the bar. A shot glass sits conspicuously on a stand in the center of the bottles. Throwing quarters at the glass, patrons try to get one in. A quarter in the glass means a free drink. Few ever stick and the bartenders get the misses as their tips. Like most bars up North, a bell hangs from the ceiling. A web of ropes is strung throughout the bar, one close to each customer. The slightest tug on the rope rings the bell, signaling a round for everybody. Many outsiders have run up incredible tabs by pulling the rope, not knowing what it meant. Mary introduces me to a couple of guys who run Thunder Cycle in Anchorage. We buy rounds and I detail my trip. They are impressed and ask about the condition of my bike, "Fine except for my brake pads."

About an hour later, coming back from the john, one says, "I called the boys at the shop, when you get into Anchorage they will have pads ready to put on your bike."

Suddenly, I look outside and see blue skies! I excitedly thank them and excuse myself. Driving all the muddy side roads in the area, I take in my first clear views of the surrounding mountains as they stab the flawless sky.

July 27, Seward

For the first time in two weeks I wake to a bright sunny morning. Leaving Seward, I head for Portage to get a ticket for the Alaskan Railroad train that runs to Whittier. I have no reason to go to Whittier, I simply want to ride the train. Other passengers are catching the ferry to Valdez.

Whittier was established by the U.S. government during WWII and is still a major tank farm where ships fuel up. The only thing of interest in Whittier is Begich Towers, a fourteen-story condominium that houses a hundred people, half of the town's population. Labeled as the "city under one roof," the building was once the largest in Alaska. With nothing to do here, I take the next available train back.

After returning to Portage, I hop on my bike and head toward Portage Lake. The U.S. Forest Service has built an incredible visitor center over part of the lake. I watch an exciting documentary, *Voices from the Ice*. As the film ends the big screen parts, revealing a huge window looking out over the iceberg decorated lake. One huge, blue chunk of ice blocks the view of the glacier that produces these icebergs.

The icebergs, varying in size from a small fist to a large house, create a scene almost too fantastic to believe. Bergs that have turned over are various shades of polished neon blue. Others are rough and stained with mud and rocks that the glacier picked up from the mountain valley. I can hear meltwater running and the occasional splash of a rock or a piece of ice plunging into the water.

After studying a map in the visitor center, I decide to hike up a valley to Byron Glacier. Unlike the Park Service, the Forest Service does not concern itself with my safety; I can hike wherever I want. Hiking on a glacier is dangerous, but I have read a little and am pretty sure of myself. Following the trail to an old terminus of the glacier, I cautiously make my way over the huge pile of boulders to the other side. The stream that the trail had followed simply flows through the rubble.

On the other side, I see where the stream entered the rocks and its source—another pile of glacial rock, the moraine. Here the stream flows out of the huge gaping mouth of a snow cave the size of a school gymnasium. I continue over the snow and onto the moraine, scrambling about half a mile up the rocks. Stopping on a ridge for lunch, I notice the sound of running water underneath. I move a few rocks, exposing glare ice. I come to the sudden realization that I am not on moraine, but actually on the glacier itself.

A rock slide had covered the ice, fooling me into thinking that I was on solid ground. Hiking far on a glacier is very dangerous, melting ice can crumble, exposing crevasses hundreds of feet deep. People have fallen into glaciers never to be heard of again. I carefully tiptoe may way back down, trying to stay on the same path, but stray. I come upon a crevasse disappearing into the bowels of the ice. I drop a rock into the dark abyss. It rattles and clanks down the chute several seconds before hitting bottom with a thud. Imagine the possibilities, hundreds of years into the future, National Geographic finds my leather clad, Harley-riding body, frozen into the glacier. "This is what people wore in the Twentieth Century." Imagine their speculation on my lifestyle. I make it back down the ice with a lot more respect for glaciers and mother nature.

On the trail back to the parking lot I meet two guys. They are wearing cheesy Australian hats and leather jackets. One carries a pump shotgun and the other has a six-pack of Coronas plus a bottle of 151 rum. Imagine National Geographic finding **them** in the ice.

I cook dinner by the edge of the lake, enjoying the peace and quiet. Suddenly, my dinner is interrupted by the loud music and yelling of the participants of an obviously drunken road trip. A cute girl walks up and asks me for a ride, I oblige and enjoy their crazy antics. I join in some frolicking but draw the line when they go for a swim in the icy waters. I don't have a warm place to go home to.

Sleeping off a side road, I am visited by many night spirits. I hear their footsteps coming through my camp. Not sure whether they might be bears or moose or something unmentionable, I decide to stay inside the false security of my tent and sleeping bag.

July 28, Portage

I get up slowly and head into Anchorage for my brake job at Thunder Cycle. I go to a car wash and clean my bike first. Few mechanics enjoy working on a dirty machine and mine is filthy. It is completely covered with a chalky layer of gray mud. First, I unload all my gear and strip the bike down to its pre-touring appearance. I spend almost an hour cleaning before I give all the chrome and painted parts a good waxing. Over two hours after my arrival I am loaded up and head to the shop. As I pull in I get a face full of the distinctive petroleum smell of wax burning, my bike's way of thanking me for the attention. Immediately I go through the stripping process again to make it easier for the mechanic to get to my bike.

I am outraged after finding out that the pads will cost $140. More Harley Inc. bullshit. They put the pads on and apologize for the price of the parts, showing me their receipt. Harley charged **them** $140!

As I wait for the work to be completed, they offer me a beer. I start to get the feeling that this is a real motorcycle shop. If it is, as closing time approaches a few regulars will start filing in for the traditional after closing beers. Like clockwork they arrive on an odd variety of classic rat bikes. Joining them for a few beers, I am flattered when these discriminating riders praise me for my trip. This place feels a little like Hollywood's, a shop I hang out at in Texas. Hollywood's seems a little scary at first, but once you get to know Hollywood and his wife/business partner—Smiles, they treat you like family. I feel sad and a little homesick when I leave Thunder, wishing I could hang out here forever.

One of the regulars says he will ride me out of town and buy me a beer on the way. To my surprize he takes me to the same bar where I met Taren. She is dancing again. As soon as she is done she puts her lacy, thong panties and bra back on and comes right over to me and plops down on my lap. My companion is obviously surprized that I know her. Giving me a kiss she says, "I'm sooo glad, you came back!" Any other time I would chalk this treatment down to salesmanship but she knows I am short on cash and not buying. Soon the bouncer comes over with a mean look on his face. She hops off my lap and onto the chair next to us. "Touching is against the rules, but I don't know why he gives a damm what we do." She gives me her real name and asks me to write to her since she is hoping to visit Texas sometime. I am surprised at her honesty, it seems to change the whole dancer/client relationship. Her motive is companionship not money and suddenly I am looking at her as a woman rather than an object. I sincerely enjoy the conversation and soon forget that she is half naked and gorgeous and only think of her as another friend. I feel guilty for ever having supported this kind of business and for throwing loonies without conscience. She walks me to my bike and gives me an affectionate hug before I hit the road.

Outside of Anchorage, I stop at a pullout to put on some warmer clothes. I notice that the moon is sitting on the horizon and moving parallel to it. If I stand very still, I can see the movement against the trees. It is slow, but sure as it gradually consumes one tree after another. I begin to imagine that I can feel the earth spinning. As I tire of watching this wonderful revelation my eyes start to wander. Scanning the landscape, I notice that this twilight is unlike anything I have seen before. The moon is illuminating the trees with a silvery glow from one side while the persistent rays of the hidden sun cast a golden glow on the other side. If I had not taken the time to focus on the moon I would have missed experiencing the motion, on the other hand if I had not sat back and taken in the whole landscape I would have missed the rich colors of the twilight. I think of traveling the same way, if you just focus on putting on miles you will miss experiences along the way. Likewise, if you stay in one place too long you will never get anywhere. A balance is necessary for a total experience.

I feel good and rested and ride till midnight with the orange half-moon hanging over the Chugach Mountains.

July 29, King Mountain

The ride east of Anchorage along the Glenn Highway to Glennallen produces excellent views of the Matanuska River framed by the persistent peaks and glaciers of the Chugach Range. The silty river has cut a deep channel exposing colorful, but unstable cliffs along its bank. The silt from this erosion gives the river a milky gray color rather that the normal glacial green. There is little traffic, making this route feel somewhat isolated.

From Glenallen I turn south toward Valdez on one of the most scenic stretches of highway in Alaska. A gust of wind blows the bandanna off my head. I double back to get it, but don't bother the put it back on. The chilly air makes my forehead throb and gives me a headache but I enjoy the cleansing flow through my hair. It is a pleasure pain combination that feels refreshing.

The scenery culminates at Thompson Pass. From this point, a conservative 2,700 feet above sea level, I am surrounded by an unbelievable vista. My eyes are led through a panorama of rugged mountains and glacial valleys to a ridge of peaks that look like the shiny teeth on a new saw. Between each tooth, melting water has cut deep canyons through smooth verdant valleys. Waterfalls are dancing everywhere.

From Thompson Pass the highway drops sharply into the city of Valdez. Valdez has the distinction of being the northernmost ice-free port in the Western Hemisphere. The original townsite was completely destroyed by the Good Friday Earthquake. The town was rebuilt on its present site in 1968.

Near the old townsite is a small stream where salmon are making a futile attempt to swim upstream. The shallow water will not allow them to swim so they flail forward cheered on by a crowd of tourists. So many people have stopped to watch this grim spectacle that the banks of the stream are hard packed and void of any vegetation. Oblivious to the entertainment that their death is providing, the fish struggle forward for several days providing food for a variety of opportunistic scavengers.

I pull into town searching for a campsite. Finding none for less than $10, I buy a warm shower at a campground before continuing my search. I stop for a beer in the Pipeline Club where Captain Hazelwood had his fateful drinks before leading the Exxon Valdez to its disaster. Finding little hospitality here, I resume my search for a campsite. Almost every person that I encounter reeks of alcohol; there must be nothing to do here other than drink. Maybe Hazelwood's intoxication was not unusual for Valdez.

On a point situated over Port Valdez sits South Harbor Campground. This rocky knoll is the site of Valdez's cannery village, pathetic compared to Homer's friendly beach community. The campground sits high above the parking lot. The edge of the site is bordered with sheer cliffs dropping into the cold sea. Signs warn, "Dangerous Cliffs." I hope nobody here sleepwalks. The hard ground will not accept stakes so tents are tied onto plywood platforms. I can't imagine that this place is any fun in a storm, sitting as high and unprotected as it is. The people here seem inhospitable and somewhat foreboding. I have an uncomfortable rest, sleeping out of sight of my bike.

July 30, Valdez

I catch the first sightseeing cruise, hoping for a repeat of the incredible experience I had in Seward. The ship is well run, but the sights do not compare with Kenai Fjords. Seals resting on icebergs and a couple bald eagles are the highlights. The site of the Exxon Valdez accident is vaguely pointed out. The view of Columbia Glacier is blocked by icebergs and heavy fog. The high point of my trip is a giddy woman who comes up to me, "Can I have my picture taken with you?" I guess a biker on a cruise in Alaska is a significant event for her.

Trying to salvage my day, I go on a tour of the Trans-Alaska Pipeline terminal. We are driven, non-stop through the terminal and tortured with a barrage of useless facts and figures. The tour guide has memorized the entire talk and leaves no pauses for questions. A recording would be as effective. I rest and make up for the sleep I lost last night.

As I decide to leave Valdez before dying of boredom, it begins to pour. Luckily, I see a sign for Valdez Glacier Campground and manage to set up camp before getting completely soaked. Signs warn, "Bears Frequent Area: Camp at Own Risk." I'm too wet and tired to care. The glacier sits high above camp. During the gold rush days, this port was marketed as a route to the gold fields by unscrupulous profiteers. The route required miners to travel over the glacier, a nearly impossible task. Many perished, their bodies lost forever in the bowels of the ice.

July 31, Valdez

As I begin my ascent to Thompson Pass, the rain turns to a mystic fog. The fog is a blessing, if I saw the incredible vista from the pass again, I'm not sure I could go any farther. In spite of the fog, I stop at the top and imagine the view, feeling its magnitude even though it is not visible.

Seventy miles up the road, I stop at the Wrangell-St. Elias National Park visitor center in Copper Center. I am drawn to the park ranger working the desk, "This is the last truly free place in our country. We have no rules, no courts, just a handful of rangers. We don't care what you do here as long as you don't break federal law. You can go in and die; we don't care."

Access to our largest national park is via a 60 mile stretch of slightly improved railway grade. The ties still remain creating nut breaking washboards and tire destroying spikes. Upon arrival in the isolated town of McCarthy, visitors must pull themselves across the Kennicott River on a small cable tram. Travelers are rewarded for their efforts with a truly wild park, complete with hundreds of unnamed peaks and glaciers. Six of the ten highest peaks in North America lie within the park boundaries. With regret I choose to leave this road to a future trip. In Glenallen, I learn that the state plans to improve the highway to McCarthy and build a bridge over the river. A road will bring more tourists and ruin the serenity of the place. I feel as if I have just missed the opportunity to witness the end of an era.

To my relief, I realize that only a very small portion of Alaska is accessible by road. I have seen only a fraction of what this state has to offer. The bulk of the wilderness is accessible only by charter planes costing hundreds of dollars. Economics are preserving most of the wilderness. It simply costs too much to get to it. Most of the mountains and valleys remain, unconcerned with man's progress. Time will tell if this will be to their benefit or demise.

As I approach Gakona Lodge a lynx darts across the road in front of me. Advertisements exclaim, "Gakona Lodge, Rustic Log, Over 60 Years Old." Sixty must be old here, Gakona is in the National Register of Historic Places. I pull in hoping to buy a meal. The restaurant is closed. The buildings look old, unpainted with weathered signs. The doors squeak. The floors creek. The ceilings sag. Out front a skinny roadhouse dog digs through the garbage looking for a snack. I am the only person here other than the owners. Wanting to support them I ask for a beer. "We have to go to the other room to sell you beer." We walk over and she quietly responds to my questions with short, simple answers. I leave, wondering how they make a living off this place.

Bartell

August 1, Tok

Back on the Alcan, I am headed for the ferry terminal in Haines. On familiar roads, I feel close to home, but it will be at least twenty days and thousands of miles before I see Texas again. I stop before crossing back into Canada to prepare myself for the stretch of construction that caused so much grief for the Californians when we came up the highway. Coping with adversity can be better done alone.

Stopping in Burwash Landing to fuel up, I decide to go inside and get a beer and lunch to celebrate the end of the ride through the construction. After the meal, I nearly fall asleep leaning on my hand. My eyes beg relief and I oblige. The darkness surrounds me, relaxing completely, I feel the blood pulsing through my veins. Slowly, the table begins to spin and I wake with a start. A family from Edmonton, Alberta sits nearby. Curious about my trip, they bombard me with a barrage of questions. I am glad to see some people who are interested in others different from themselves. Through their example, these parents are teaching their children to appreciate diversity.

Back along the highway, the scenery seems less impressive than the first time I drove it. Seasonal fires have obscured the mountains with a heavy layer of smoke. The haze intensifies the sun's strain on my eyes. The combination of the construction, the beer, and the haze tires me. I find a nice campground in Kluane National Park and take a short hike. Along the trail an old black and red BMW is chained to a tree. Mounted on top of the handle bars is a blue mannequin head. Obviously, an individual's ride. The rider must be out hiking the wilderness.

An interpretive sign announces the shore of Lake Kathleen. It explains the life cycle of Kokono Salmon. These salmon were landlocked in this lake by a glacial landslide thousands of years ago. With their natural life cycle disrupted and unable to go to the sea, they have adapted to this lake. They now complete their entire life cycle in this network of freshwater lakes and streams. I wonder if they realize their loss and feel a longing for the sea each year or are they content to live in this sheltered habitat? I realize how lucky I am to be able to travel the world as freely as I do.

August 2, Kathleen Lake, Yukon Territory

On my way to Haines, I stop at a small fishing village called Klukshu. The town is composed of numerous small, unpainted shacks, many without electricity. They are squat, I would have to duck to go through any of the doors. Most are built from twisted logs. They have all settled into the ground, finding their own unlevel foundation on the front heaves. The village has no organization. The shacks are haphazardly strewn across the meadow. As I pull through, a couple of old men sitting on a bench in front of their house catch my eye. Their weathered faces look as rugged and creased as the surrounding mountains. Maybe, as they age, they assimilate the mountains into their faces the way a couple growing old together eventually look alike, taking on each other's appearance through shared experience. I stop and greet them. Showing me their salmon traps, they talk of annual salmon runs and the bears that steal their catch. Displaying the dogs that help defend the traps, they tell how the dogs warn them when a bear comes near and fight to the death if the grizz gets too close. These people have chosen a hard, but simple life away from the stresses of the modern world. Unlike the Indians in the States, they have made a choice to live on their homeland as they please. In the States, few tribes were allowed to stay on their homeland. Most were juggled around to worthless lands. They now rely on government checks for their survival. The native people here can survive independently as long as the salmon keep coming.

The smooth highway runs from the Yukon through a thin piece of British Columbia before ending in Alaska. The 120 mile stretch from Haines Junction to Klukwan is the longest distance I travel without a service station. Near the border, some bikers from Iowa have realized that they don't have enough gas to make it. They turn around hoping to make it back to Haines Junction. For about thirty miles the highway travels through the tundra above timber line. Before beginning the descent into Haines, I stop at Three Guardsmen Pass. The view down the valley varies from rock and glacier, to dry tundra, to coastal rain forest at the bottom. Rising starkly in the west, the Takhinsha

Mountains look as if they were drawn by a small child. Perfect triangular peaks capped in white snow reach for the blue sky.

Crossing back into the U.S., I am thrown off guard by a border officer who is friendly. He greets me with a smile, I am suspicious. We talk not about what I'm carrying or where I'm going, but rather, "How about this sunny weather?" and, "How about that view from the pass?" I keep thinking it is some sort of trick. Aren't border guards supposed to treat you with suspicion and make you feel like a criminal? Maybe not.

The highway descends along the wide sluggish Chilkat River, through the Chilkat Eagle Preserve. This area is famous for its concentrations of bald eagles. More than 3,000 of the scavengers spend the winter here living off an unusually late run of salmon. The salmon have found a warm spring where they can spawn as late as January. The eagles live off their remains. Eagles are so common here that after a couple days here you no longer notice them.

Descending into Haines, I find a camping site at the Bear Creek Hostel. Five dollars a night with showers and a kitchen with cooking utensils and a refrigerator. I decide to stay a while. The owners of the hostel, Ron, Rhett, and Geraldine, show me incredible hospitality, even cooking me dinner a couple nights. They have just bought the hostel and are encountering numerous problems left by the previous owners. All the records of past reservations have been lost. They have no idea who has reserved what, when. They manage to maintain a welcome environment in spite of all the difficulties they are facing.

August 3, Haines, Alaska

I wake up and take a shower, two days in a row! Hoping to find a water taxi to Skagway, I ride into town. Haines is 13 miles by water but 350 miles by road, from Skagway. The highway was built in 1978, before then train, plane, and boat were the only way to get to Skagway. I stop at a travel agency and inquire about trips to Skagway, $30 round trip on the water taxi, or $60 by plane. I decide to split the difference and fly one way and float home, $45. The travel agent is legally blind but still working—admirable. Later I see him driving a moped around town. He says he can see the road and the movement of oncoming cars. Most of the locals just stay out of his way.

This town reminds me so much of the small towns in South Dakota where I grew up, that it is almost scary. The bars on Main Street outnumber the grocery stores two to one. People are friendly and start recognizing me after my second day here. The visitors who arrive by ferry rarely stay and those who arrive by road usually leave on the next departing ferry. The Chilkat Indian word for the site was simply, "End of the Trail." The only time any number of people stay is during the Alaskan State Fair which draws a considerable crowd. My schedule forces me to leave a day before the fair starts. Due south of town, the buildings of Fort Seward sit boldly looking over the harbor. Most of these massive buildings have been converted into homes, but one contains an Indian museum and art center and another has become a hotel and restaurant.

The airport in Haines is one of the busiest I have ever seen, planes constantly taking off and landing. At least four different flying services operate out of this airfield. We are shuttled from town and drive right out onto the runway where we wait for the plane to pick us up. Soon he lands and taxis up next to us. We fly a single engine Cessna to Skagway. The pilot gives me "shotgun." I sit next to the him with a set of pedals and controls right in front of me. I am able to figure out what several of the gauges on the dash are. An altimeter holds my attention as we take off, rising quickly above the runway and I am tempted to grab the controls and try to take the plane through a series of acrobatic maneuvers. I always wanted to be a fighter pilot, but my eyes went bad when I was ten. The flight lasts about ten minutes and wets my appetite for more time in the air. I make a mental note to look into a flightseeing tour when I get back to Haines.

I walk to the nearest campground and set up my tent before heading into town. Skagway is a tourist trap if I have ever seen one. During the winter, the population of the town is less than half what it is now. During the summer, the town becomes a conglomeration of gift shops disguised as old fashioned stores complete with costumed clerks. With three cruise ships anchored in the port, the town is a frenzy of old ladies buying tourist crap and old men sitting on benches in front of the shops waiting. I am writing in my journal when an old guy sits next to me. He moans, "It's terrible to grow old."

I don't know why he doesn't keep his misery to himself. Life is what you make of it, old or young. I don't know what he wants so I don't respond. I acknowledge him only in my journal.

I slide into the Red Onion Saloon for a cold one. As I am enjoying my brew, I recognize two women from the campground and I offer them the stools next to me. They accept. A pleasant pair of "Anns." Marianne is from Seattle and Lea Ann turns out to be from Texas. Leigh Ann seems shy and reserved at first but Marianne has a large confident air about her. She has a rugged attractive quality that reminds me of the outdoors and makes me feel at home. They have been working for the Forest Service on Sitka Island. This is their final weekend off before their seasonal jobs end and they have to return home. We go back to the campground and enjoy a quiet evening around a cozy campfire.

August 4, Skagway

I join Marianne and Lea Ann for a hike on the Skyline Trail. The trail follows the backbone of a ridge leading to a high peak just above the city. As we hike, I imagine the Klondike miners who landed in town and began their ascent up Chilkoot Pass on a trail not far from here. Embarking on the rugged journey to the gold fields in the Yukon, they were required to bring over a ton of supplies with them to survive the harsh conditions in the North country. Many had no pack animals and had to carry all the cargo on their backs; a task which required numerous trips up the steep pass. I only have a couple water bottles and a small lunch, but the trail is still strenuous.

The hike takes us through numerous patches of blueberries and salmonberries. The lunch I packed is unnecessary since we gorge ourselves on the feast of berries that mother nature hands us. About halfway up the mountain we take a long break discussing the sadness we all feel as we near the end of our time in Alaska. We also share our turmoil over the pressures from family and society, trying to force us to choose an occupation and settle down. None of us has committed to a career. We all like living with uncertainty. I have to head back down to catch my ferry, but the girls continue on.

I pack up and head to the docks. Along the way down Main Street, I notice that men and women who were dressed in miner costumes and cat house dresses yesterday, are now wearing jeans and T-shirts. No cruise ships to impress today.

On the trip back to Haines the wind suddenly picks up and before too long it starts to rain. Our small ferry is tossed back and forth. Water is blowing over the bow. The observation deck is getting drenched with airborne waves, forcing me to go inside to stay dry. The trip that normally takes about 45 minutes lasts almost two hours in the heavy headwinds. I worry about the girls, still up on the mountain. I find out later that they got lost, but eventually found their way back down—wet but unharmed.

Back in Haines, I see a familiar BMW with a blue head, the same bike that was parked at Kathleen Lake chained to a tree. I do a quick U-turn, eager to meet the eccentric. He is leaning on his bike, gorging himself on fried chicken from the grocery store deli. His heavy, dark features hide in the shadow of his long black hair. A large backpack is strapped to the back of his bike. Mike is from New York, originally. He has been traveling for about a month, starting in California. I will find out later that his trip turns into a nightmare with numerous breakdowns and blowouts; one causing a wreck that nearly totals his bike in Montana. We share a few of our adventures and then wish each other luck.

Cooking dinner back at the hostel, I hear a knock on the kitchen door. It is Mike. He wants to come over tomorrow to cook breakfast and then go on a fifteen mile mega-hike. I accept the challenge.

August 5, Haines

Mike doesn't show, so I go into town, looking for something to see or do. I see him at the Air Service trying to return a COD package. UPS doesn't seem to understand that he can't give the package back to the driver. There was no driver. The package was flown here, from Seattle, by the local air service. They won't fly it back unless UPS picks up the bill. After a couple hours on the phone, he gets his problem solved and we plan an evening hike up Mount Ripley.

I meet Mike at the McDonald's, a local family that has agreed to put him up for a couple nights. They have just been out on the bay checking their crab traps. We feast on fresh king crab. We carefully wash our hands before heading up the mountain, not wanting to attract any bears with the smell of fresh seafood. Rumor has it that a girl was treed last night on the trail we are taking.

A perfect pair of boisterous conversationalists, Mike and I tell our life stories and solve most of the world's problems before we reach the summit. Soon the trees begin to shrink and twist, malformed by intense winter winds, turning the forest into a natural bonsai garden. A high marsh is crossed by 2X6s propped inches above the shallow water. I imagine that this bridge is a dangerous test of balance at the entrance to a fantasy land. We make it across the bridge and climb to the summit. Watching the sunset over the Lynn Canal, we can see the line where the fresh waters of the Chilkat are mixing with the saltwater from the advancing tide. Mesmerized by the sunset, we forget that we have to hike back down the steep trail. We make enough noise through our conversation to alert any bears that might be along the trail. In spite of our loud voices, the night forest forces its sober mood upon us. We stop for a break and soon find ourselves sitting in silence. This is an unsettling contrast to Texas where the forest comes alive with the deafening sounds of nocturnal insects and frogs. The density of the old growth blocks the remaining light, producing a total darkness that I have not experienced for several weeks. It is a slightly disturbing, but welcome change.

119

August 6, Haines

Seeing the valley from the top of Mount Ripley reminded me of flightseeing tours of the area. I discover that they vary from $100 to $150 per person per hour. Way out of my price range. Finally, I find a charter service that has planes for $250 per hour with five passenger seats. I go around town soliciting people to join me on this bargain flight. Walking down the street I discover Chris, the German on the dirt bike who rode up the Alcan with me. He joins my flight along with another German, a French woman, and a Canadian woman. I think that makes this an international flight!

The flight is spectacular, I expected more climbs and dives, but the pilot keeps the plane at an even 1,400 feet for most of the flight. We follow Daniel's Glacier up over the divide and into Glacier Bay National Park. Once over the park, we fly above several glaciers and buzz huge rocks defiantly sticking out of the snowcap. The lakes below reflect a thousand shades of blue and green, complimenting the colors of the glacial ice. Seeing a glacier from the air reveals long flowing patterns making the slow movement of the ice obvious.

Too soon the flight is over. Few words have been spoken, as no comments were called for. Words can not express the feelings brought forth by such beauty. Except for the drone of the engine, we have flown in complete silence.

I get together with several of the guests from the hostel and go for an evening hike at Chilkat State Park. Carefully picking my way over the slick silt covered rocks, I notice for the first time that I have never before seen a beach without man's garbage. The word pristine comes to mind.

A spectacular sunset reflecting off the Chilkat forces us to stop on the way home. We watch the sun slowly slide sideways across the horizon, gradually angling into it rather than just dropping below it as in lower latitudes. The deep colors of the sunset remind me of the rich aged paint on a fine antique. The memory of the moon outside of Anchorage echos in my mind. Some local children have also come to watch the end of the day. One boy walks with me as I set up the perfect angle for a photo.

"If this picture turns out you could sell it to the postcard company." He is right, I probably could. I will send him a copy.

Rhett cooks me dinner back at the hostel, barbecue chicken. I have noticed that he seems to be working his ass off while Ron and Geri take care of the office. Ron and Rhett had come up to Alaska a couple months earlier, hoping to escape life in the Lower Forty-eight. On the ferry Ron met Geri and they immediately hit it off. Geri shared her plans to take over this small hostel and try to make a living. By the end of the trip they had decided to go into it together. Rhett had thought he was a partner with them, but has turned into their handy man. He came to Alaska looking for paradise and is now cleaning toilets. He takes no time to appreciate the beauty of the place in which he lives. Spending all of his spare time worrying about his future, he wastes the present.

August 7, Haines

Forced to go into town by the theft of my toilet kit from the hostel showerhouse, I spend the morning buying a toothbrush and all the other necessities for my hygiene. On the way back to the campsite, I notice a couple of bikers sitting by a picnic table. The man is riding a new Harley Evolution mounted on a rigid frame. Modified with a kickstart and hand shift this is not a motorcycle, it's a chopper. His wife is running a Sportster with baling wire holding the footpegs and mufflers together. They chose to ride up the shorter but rougher Cassiar Highway rather than the Alcan. The long stretches of gravel and washboards have taken a toll on their bikes. The man is dressed in bib overalls and a canvas jacket. Unconcerned with his appearance, he looks more like a farmer than a biker. We end up talking for several hours. While we put down Yuppies and RUBs, an old couple on a shiny new Harley FLH pull up; a complete dresser. I quickly judge them as tourists rather than travelers. I couldn't have been more wrong. The have both passed seventy and have been riding more than thirty years. More than half a million miles later they still love the highway. They tell us about "Hard Core." They rode the Alcan in 1970. Then the road was mostly gravel and muddy ruts. In those days fuel stops were not as frequent and they had to carry extra gas. I swallow my pride and recognize "True Grit." I wish the old man who sat next to me in Skagway and told me that growing old is terrible could see this couple growing old.

"A man is not old as long as he is seeking something."
-Jean Rostand

Back at the hostel, I am in the kitchen cooking my dinner when a group of other guests comes in. I am not feeling social so I mind my own business. A woman from Vancouver looks at me and remarks, "Let's take a picture, a guy is actually cooking!" She doesn't know me so I ignore her ignorant insult, but it is not her last. She criticizes me for hiking after dark in bear country. "You're lucky you didn't get eaten the other night." Later that night after criticizing seatbelt laws because the belts are "too constricting," she finally confronts me about my choice to ride without a helmet. Not realizing the hypocrisy of her opinion, she tells me, "You're crazy not to wear a helmet." Pushed beyond my limit, I explode and tell her that I don't need her or any other hypocrite to look after my safety. Others sitting around the campfire laugh at her obvious discomfort.

"You can not subvert your neighbor's rights
without striking a dangerous blow to your own."
-Carl Shurz.

Shortly before we go to bed, a strange dog comes into camp. The black lab heads right for Ron's huge pet, Ben. Ben is an Akita Inu, a type of dog bred in Japan for killing bears. At first we think nothing of having a visitor in camp. Both dogs start prancing around, growling from deep within their chests. Ron and Rhett try to keep the dogs apart but soon they are locked together in a frenzy of rips and flying hair. Suddenly, the lab has ahold of Ben's throat. We manage to pry the dogs apart and keep the lab from slicing Ben's jugular. The climate here seems to bring out the wild in both dogs and people. Everybody seems friendly and hospitable, but I get the feeling that if you invade anybody's space you will find trouble.

August 8, Haines

My last day in Haines. Planning to make the best of it, I head down the Mud Bay Road to Chilkat State Park for an early morning hike. I spend lots of time sitting, trying to permanently etch the views into my mind. The bay, with seals catching fish and playing in the surf, sits behind the foreground of old growth forest and pristine beaches. Sitting in a saddle in the surrounding mountains is Rainbow Glacier. The mass of ice is perched precariously on a shear cliff at what seems like a thousand feet above the water. Even from this distance I hear, or at least imagine I can hear, the roar of the waterfalls hanging from the ice. I quietly head back to the hostel for lunch.

After eating, I take some time to repair some patches that are falling off my jacket. The trip has taken a toll on my gear and my bike. My tour pack is falling apart at the rivets, the gas tank has numerous nicks and scratches, a flying rock has split the windshield, and the weight of my gear pounding on the rear fender has bent it, creasing both sides. I use some baling wire to fasten the load to the frame to take some of the weight off the fender. Sitting in the direct sunlight, I am quickly overheated; the sun's rays sucking the energy out of me. Moving under a tree for a nap, I am quickly cooled by the shade. The contrast between sun and shade is apparent. This 80 degree weather has the locals worried about heat stroke. They are not accustomed to it. They would surely die in Texas.

Planning to finish the day with a hike to Battery Point, I leave my bike and start walking. It is perfect. Nobody is on the trail. Preparing to leave Alaska tomorrow on the ferry, I need time to myself. I find a nice rock leaning out into the bay and climb onto it. Sitting here for several hours I find peace in the solitude. As the sun hangs on to the horizon a school of porpoises comes and frolics nearby, begging me to join them. I hike back to my bike, ready to end my day with the memory of this perfect evening etched in my mind forever.

August 9, Haines

My ferry trip south departs today. I bid farewell to Ron, Geri, and Rhett. Throughout town the locals are splitting firewood. Stacks are piling up in every yard in preparation for the winter that is quickly approaching. A winter that I am escaping. Showing up at the terminal early to confirm my reservation, I am greeted by the woman at the entrance, "You must be Allen!" She responds to the surprised look on my face, "We have only one motorcycle reservation. Go right up to the front of the line." I like this kind of service.

I will be riding the Alaskan Marine Highway on the *Malaspina* all the way to Prince Rupert, British Columbia. A 36 hour trip that would take about four days by road. It costs a reasonable $200 for myself and my bike for the cruise that will take me through Alaska's scenic Inside Passage. The trip is worth the price for the sights alone.

The *Malaspina* is not a fancy ship, even though it may have been at one time. The common areas are all showing their wear from continuous use. I head for the covered solarium near the back of the boat, hoping to find a lounge chair to crash in since I didn't buy a sleeping room. Passengers who boarded at Skagway have already claimed all the functional chairs. I find one that won't sit up and wedge it against a pillar. Intense yellow light radiates through the clear yellow panels that form the canopy and three sides of this deck. The area has one side completely exposed to the elemements. We have an unrestricted view, looking back toward the wake left by our large vessel. This large opening does not provide enough fresh air and I am soon parched. Kicking back with a case of Luckies that I smuggled onto the ship, I feel like a juvenile delinquent. I pour my first beer under the cover of my sleeping bag. Drinks are not allowed anywhere but the lounge, where they charge $3.50 per draw. Passengers used to be allowed to bring their own, but the resulting brawls and vandalism forced the state to ban public consumption on the ship.

Near the front of the vessel is a large sitting room with a panorama of windows looking forward over the path of the ship. This observatory is the stage for U.S. Forest Service employee, Steve

Clarkson, who offers informative programs on the natural and cultural history of the surrounding communities. He manages to present some relatively boring information in an entertaining manner. At one point he recites *The Cremation of Sam McGee* from memory. I especially enjoy his opinions on the uses and abuses of the surrounding ecosystems. As we travel south clear cutting of the ancient forests becomes more and more common. I feel sorrow and shame for these scars on the landscape. I am sobered by the sight of the terrible impact of every sheet of paper I have ever wasted. We are all guilty. Clarkson comments, "If we can't replace these old growth forests in our lifetime, can we consider them a renewable resource?"

Steve's programs, along with a Tom Bodett book, casually pull me through the less exciting portions of the trip. Between the programs and my naps, wonderful views of the mountains rise out of the narrow waterway. Smoke from fires as far away as Idaho is paling the views, destroying their photographic qualities, so they are committed to memory. Dolphins and humpback whales play in the wake of the ship. I watch diligently and am finally rewarded with a glimpse of a pack or "pod" of killer whales hunting. Seeing these animals at Sea World is a Walt Disney view of their lifestyle. Swimmers play in the water with these trained pets like a lion tamer plays with his beasts. In the wild these mammals offer a much more honest and haunting picture. They are ruthless and efficient predators of seals, but have been known to attack anything including polar bears and other whales. They sometimes beach themselves, coming completely out of the water to snap a small seal off the beach. They then play with the seal, tossing it back and forth, before finally devouring it. The food chain is a simple fact of survival in the emotionless natural world. Playing with prey before eating it must have some purpose that I can not begin to understand.

Sitting in the chairs next to me are two cute girls, Rebecca and Susan from Vancouver. Their round faces are decorated with freckles and sunny smiles. You could mistake them for sisters. At first they view me from a distance. Eventually, I break the ice with a warm smile and some cheese and crackers. They have spent their summer working at a hotel in Whitehorse. They rode their bicycles 100 miles down the Klondike Highway to Skagway where they boarded the ship. They are on their way home to Vancouver where they attend the University of British Columbia.

We arrive in Juneau under a setting sun. Mendenhall Glacier reflects an eerie combination of glacier blue mixed with blood red from the smoky sunset. Juneau, the capital of Alaska, is about 200 miles south of Haines. Isolated by the Coast Mountains, Juneau has no access by highway. Visitors arrive either by ferry or by air. Due to lack of funding, the city remains the capitol despite several attempts to move it to a more centrally located site. Government comprises half of the total industry in the city. We waste no time here, getting underway as soon as all the cars are loaded and the empty spaces are filled with truck trailers full of supplies bound for ports to the south.

Sleeping under the lights of the ship, surrounded by about a hundred other passengers doesn't bother me as much as I expect. A combination of the progression of the season and southerly travel produces a couple hours of complete darkness. The lights are eventually shut off and the windows of the solarium allow the stars to peek through. I doze off easily, snuggled in my warm bag on a comfortable lounge chair, soothed by the warm rumble of the ship's engines.

August 10, Petersburg, Alaska

I wake as the Captain announces our arrival in Petersberg, about 200 miles south of Juneau. Some other bikers boarded at Juneau. Kevin is from North Carolina, Michael is from California, and Mike and Neil are from Dawson Creek, British Columbia. Mike and Neil appear to be serious bikers with their worn leathers and sober expression. Neil hardly says a word, just sits back and nods his head in agreement with most of Mike's comments. Mike has a full head of hair and beard. He is a large man with a pensive look that is hard to read. The Canadians' Harleys appear to be dirty, but well maintained, work horses compared to Michael and Kevin's shiny Softails. In contrast to the Canadians, Michael and Kevin appear to be clean cut, white collar, lighthearted and outgoing. Kevin is trying to look tough, but doesn't quite pull it off. Michael is an all around nice guy. You couldn't find a reason to dislike him if you tried. We spend the afternoon in the warm sunlight trading my contraband beers for Jack Daniel's coolers.

A short stop in Wrangell gives me the opportunity to get off the ship and stretch my legs on solid ground. The docks are covered with local children peddling garnets and offering guided walks to the beaches where petroglyphs are carved into large boulders. Half of the kids disappear when they find out that we won't be here long enough for a walk on the beach. On trips to Mexico I have always had a weakness for children peddling souvenirs, buying things I don't need out of sympathy. Here, with the kids looking more well off than most, I have little sympathy and feel obligated to buy no rocks.

Upon our arrival in Ketchikan, the Captain announces a six hour layover in this, our last port in Alaska. We are able to convince the steward to let us take our bikes off to cruise the town. To my disappointment, my bike is packed in too tightly to move. Having already invited Susan and Rebecca along for a ride, I am now forced to be a passenger myself. Rebecca rides with Mike, Susan rides with Kevin, and I ride with Neil. He has a stripped AMF Super Glide and I enjoy the unfamiliar experience as a passenger. He would rather have one of the girls.

Ketchikan is a long narrow ribbon of a town; the many buildings of its business district held above the waterfront by a forest of pilings driven into the water below. Many of the residences are hidden on the mountainsides above the winding streets. Long treacherous stairways are the only access to many. Riding down the main drag I feel like a child, intimidated by a long dark hallway. The muggy streets of this city receive over 14 feet of precipitation each year. Local residents rarely have to worry about sunburn.

Easily finding the nearest biker bar, we are given a guided tour of all of the roads this isolated town has to offer by some of the locals. The thirty mile strip of highway reveals some excellent views of the surrounding rainforests. The girls, excited about their first rides on Harleys, force us to stop several times along the way to record the event on film. We watch the crimson rays of the setting sun ricochet off the glassy waters of a small bay. Back in town, we hit the bars hard and show the girls a great time. Several pitchers later we head back to the ship. With about fifteen minutes to spare, the steward is a little upset. Neil says I rode like dead weight, drunk and leaning all the wrong ways. My feet, weighted by the beer, fall heavily on the narrow metal stairways of the ship as I stagger to the solarium. I stumble to my chair and pass out.

August 11, Prince Rupert, British Columbia

The blinding lights come on. The captain's voice blares out of the speakers, "We will be docking in Prince Rupert at 5:00 am, please have all of your belongings packed and be ready to unload."

The watch on a lifeless hand next to me says 3:00 am. My head is pounding. Passing out on the moving ship has produced an extreme hangover. It will stay with me all day. I try to fall back to sleep, but the lights stay on and people all around me are packing up. I finally give up, pack my bike and relax beside it until we are ready to get off.

Following the advice of the British Colombians I met in South Dakota, I go immediately to the B.C. ferry terminal and get on the reserve list. The ferry to Vancouver Island will be leaving very shortly, at 7:30. They fit all the bikes on before we head toward Port Hardy on the *Queen of the North*. This ship puts the Alaskan ferries to shame. It is modern and shows little wear. The sitting room is spacious with a full service bar and game room. Later in the afternoon, the staff will operate bars throughout the ship. Not in the mood for any more beers, I mill around, exploring all of the facilities. Susan and Rebecca are aboard, watching a movie. I sit with them and sleep off my hangover. After waking, several hours later, I am invited to Vancouver but I save their offer for another time.

The mountains become less striking and we see no more glaciers. Scenes that would leave most people in awe seem ordinary after all that I have experienced. The ship's route takes us through some unbelievably narrow passages. At one point I can see flowers growing beneath huge cedars on both sides of the ship. The passage is less than 200 yards wide. Out of Alaska, with less than two weeks before I have to be back in Texas, the end of my journey is pulling me. I sit alone most of the afternoon, preparing myself for civilization. The ship docks on Vancouver Island just before midnight.

August 12, Port Hardy, British Columbia

Kevin is still with me as we head down the island, there is little traffic so we run hard, 70-80 miles per hour, hardly taking time to notice the scenery. Kevin rides like he wants to get somewhere. Used to a more casual pace, I struggle to keep up with him as he passes the trains of cars we come upon.

Too soon, we are in Campbell River, halfway down the island. At first, this town seems like most of the lazy towns throughout the North, then we pass through a busy intersection and find ourselves in the middle of civilization complete with traffic jams, construction, and the impatient honks of frustrated drivers. Not having prepared myself for this insanity, I feel like a scared rabbit, trapped and wanting nothing other than to get out of here.

At Parksville, we head across the island toward Pacific Rim National Park. We make it to the park at sunset and watch the day end before heading into Ucluelet for a few beers to wind us down. We find a sleazy hotel bar, get a table, and are immediately joined by several Indian women, none of whom could be considered attractive. Soon, we are the center of attention, with people pulling up tables to join ours. Two men seem to be in competition to be ringleaders of this clan. The smaller of the two reminds me of Popeye, skinny with a scarred face. The other could be Brutus's double. He is overweight with unkept hair and a straggly beard. A dirty tee-shirt clings to his gut and his loose sweatpants leave half of his ass-crack exposed. Expecting a quiet night in the woods, I am uncomfortable with the uninvited advances of these locals. They offer us a place to set up our tents and Kevin accepts without consulting me.

We follow a beat up Chevy truck to a dilapidated two-story house with a variety of junked cars decorating the yard. "You can set up your tents here," says 'Popeye' as he points to a bare spot with a couple piles of dog shit.

I find myself standing alone surveying the camping spot. Soon I follow everybody into the house without setting up the tent. Inside I am greeted with a rolled dollar bill and a line of cocaine. Declining the offer, I am eyed with suspicion by all in the room. I escape the

131

uncomfortable situation by telling them I am tired and just want to go to sleep. From outside, I can hear Brutus's voice rise above all the laughter, "What's his problem. . . He's probably a cop! If he's a cop he's not leaving here alive!"

I decide to go back inside to try to reassure everyone of my intentions, "I don't do coke and I just want a quiet night's sleep."

"You don't do coke? Do you want to fuck my wife?" he points to his toothless companion.

"No thanks, that's not my thing."

"You don't want to fuck her?" he smiles, "Do you want to fuck me?" He turns around and drops his pants baring his hairy ass.

If he was trying to get rid of me, it worked, I jump on my bike and leave Kevin with them. I find a restless night's sleep along Kennedy Lake, wondering why they couldn't respect my choice.

August 13, Ucluelet, British Columbia

I try to find some solitude and peace in the area, but am bombarded with crowds of tourists and sluggish traffic jams. The forests that have not been clear-cut are full of hikers and families struggling to enjoy this place. No part of the island appears untouched as so much of Alaska did. The very qualities that bring people to the wilderness are being destroyed by the people who seek their refuge here. It may only be a matter of time before all of this comes and takes over Alaska.

I find a small park with an old growth forest called Cathedral Grove. Sitting under a colossal 800 year old fir, I feel like crying for all that has been lost here. I roll my trip around in my head; I have created a small adventure, have discovered "pristine," and have seen whatever was offered to me. I have been blessed with an experience that is available nowhere else. I realize that most people will live their whole life without even having a taste of the freedom that I have experienced these past weeks.

I ride to Nanaimo to catch a ferry to the border crossing outside of Vancouver. I arrive at the terminal with near perfect timing, only a five minute wait. Parked next to me are five Hell's Angels MC bikes. As our ferry approaches, they come back to their rides. Spotting the unusual patches on my back, they come for a closer look. They move on, seeing that I'm no threat to them or their territory. Waiting to get on the ship, they rev their engines and lurch ahead impatiently like wild horses caught in a corral. As soon as the steward drops his hand, they tear out, quickly disappearing into the bowels of the ship. The thunder of their machines echoes through the hull like the roar of a dragon defiantly defending its lair. I wonder if they are really wild and free or just putting on a show.

Sitting on the ferry that will take me back to the "Lower 48" with traffic jams, uptight cops, and all the stresses of my "real" life, I realize that nobody here knows what I have just done or where I have been. I want to stand up and shout, "I just rode this bike to Alaska! Sixty days and 12,000 miles! Camping along the road!" Figuring that nobody would really care or understand, I sit quietly, but proudly on my bike while everybody else goes to the observation deck. I realize now that, as Ken Welsh said,

> "Real traveling is not just the chance to say that you've been to a place, but the feeling that at one time, somewhere, even if only for an instant, you feel like you have become a part of the land through which you traveled."

The Road North

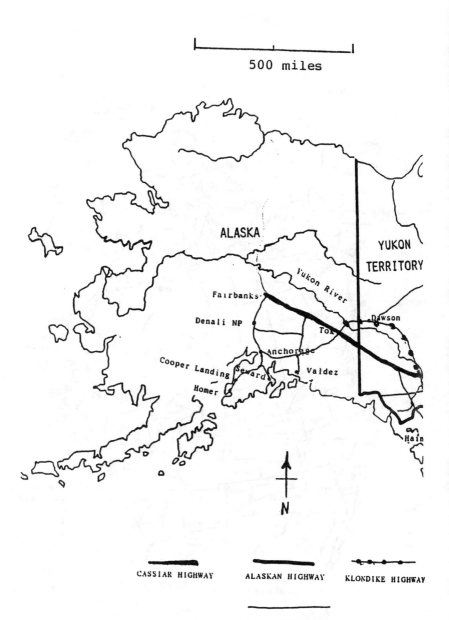

500 miles

ALASKA

YUKON
TERRITORY

Yukon River

Fairbanks

Denali NP

Dawson

Tok

Cooper Landing

Anchorage

Seward

Valdez

Homer

Hain

N

CASSIAR HIGHWAY   ALASKAN HIGHWAY   KLONDIKE HIGHWAY

Other Highways

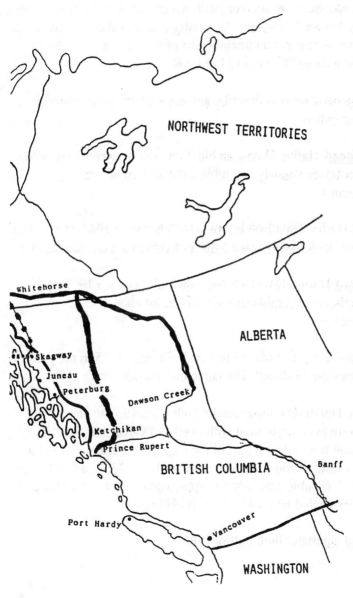

NORTHWEST TERRITORIES

ALBERTA

Whitehorse

Skagway

Juneau

Peterburg

Dawson Creek

Ketchikan

Prince Rupert

BRITISH COLUMBIA

Banff

Port Hardy

Vancouver

WASHINGTON

137

Glossary of Motorcycle Terms

Big Twin-Line of engines built by Harley Davidson, introduced in 1936 and continuing to survive (with major modifications) to present day. They have a 45 degree "V" configuration and overhead valves. The transmission is not an integral part of the engine. Usually designated with an "F" i.e. FLH or FXR.

V-Twin-generic term to describe any engine with a two cylinder "V" configuration.

Knucklehead-Harley-Davidson big twin built between 1936-1947. The rocker boxes vaguely resemble a fist. (61 cubic inch displacement.)

Panhead-Harley-Davidson big twin built between 1948-1965. The rockerboxes look like inverted pans. (74 cubic inch displacement.)

Shovelhead-Harley-Davidson big twin built between 1966-1984. The rockerboxes resemble shovels. (74 or 80 cubic inch displacement.)

Evolution-Harley-Davidson big twin built from 1985 to the present. Sometimes called E-heads. (80 cubic inch displacement.)

Sportster-Harley-Davidson model built from 1957 to the present. Has the V-twin configuration with overhead valves but the transmission is an integral part of the engine. Generally 883 cubic centimeter displacement but also made in 1000, 1100, and 1200 cc models. (1200 cubic centimeter is approximately 74 cubic inches.) Usually designated with an "X" i.e. XLH883

Ironhead-Sportster built before 1985.

Chopper-Any motorcycle that has been heavily modified but especially with regards to the front end. Many are raked (increasing the angle between the front forks and the frame) and stretched (increasing the length of the forks.) This pushes the front wheel away from the motorcycle.

Drag Pipes-Exhaust pipes without a muffler. Legal only for racing applications but are prevalent among Harley riders. This gives the bikes the deep loud sound we are all familiar with.

Dresser-Any motorcycle that has touring accessories, especially fiberglass tour packs, windshields, and fairings.

Drive-Mechanism that gives power to the rear wheel some bikes have a shaft drive. Harleys usually are equipped with a chain but newer models have a Kevlar belt.

Primary Drive-Mechanism that brings power from the engine to the transmission, usually in the form of a chain.

Rigid Frame-Frame which has no suspension holding the rear wheel. The wheel is attached directly to the frame which yields a relatively rough ride but enhances the look of the bike and cuts the weight considerably. Sometimes called a hardtail.

Rocker Box-Located at the top of each cylinder on the engine. It covers the rockers, shafts, valve stems, and valve springs.

Softail-Frame with the rear suspension hidden within the frame. Has the look of a rigid frame with the ride of a swingarm.

Swingarm-Mechanism that holds the rear wheel, it is attached to the frame but pivots and has a shock absorber system.